CHIEF EXECUTIVE ALLIANCE

# Leadership Series with World's #1 CEO Coach Mark Thompson

With more than 10 million copies sold and based on more than 10,000 hours of research, we want to thank you for your generous support for these three game-changing bestsellers. As a result of this groundbreaking work, we have built the C-Suite's most exclusive community known as The Chief Executive Alliance. We would like to invite you to participate at www.ChiefExecutiveAlliance.com

**ADMIRED**
21 WAYS TO DOUBLE YOUR VALUE

MARK C. THOMPSON
BONITA S. THOMPSON

# ADMIRED

## 21 WAYS TO
## DOUBLE YOUR VALUE

MARK C. THOMPSON
DR. BONITA S. THOMPSON, ED.D, MBA

Copyright © 2022 Mark Thompson & Dr. Bonita Thompson
All rights reserved.
ISBN: 9798447316310

To Vanessa, our BFF,
who taught us a new kind of love
that has changed our lives

# Contents

Foreword by Frances Hesselbein & Marshall Goldsmith ................................................ vi

Acknowledgments ........................................................................................................ x

### Section I
## What You Want

Chapter 1: Are You Valued? ........................................................................................ 17

Chapter 2: How to Become an MVP ............................................................................ 23

Chapter 3: Create Your Portfolio of Priorities ............................................................ 29

Chapter 4: Define What Success Means ..................................................................... 37

Chapter 5: The Law of Distraction ............................................................................. 45

Chapter 6: The Passion Trap ...................................................................................... 53

### Section II
## What They Want

Chapter 7: Everyone Sees Value Differently .............................................................. 63

Chapter 8: The Power of Praise .................................................................................. 69

Chapter 9: Finding Common Ground ........................................................................... 75

### Section III
## What To Do—A D M I R E

Chapter 10: **ACTION** ................................................................................................. 85

Tool #1 Don't Wait to Be Asked ............................................................. 87

Tool #2 Create Value .............................................................................. 92

Tool #3 Guilt is Good ............................................................................ 102

Tool #4 The Right Tool For The Job ...................................................... 107

Chapter 11: **DEVELOP** ............ 113

     Tool #5 Start Where You Are ............ 114

     Tool #6 Invest in Yourself ............ 117

     Tool #7 Live What You Are For ............ 122

     Tool #8 Be Misunderstood ............ 127

Chapter 12: **MEASURE** ............ 131

     Tool #9 How to Sabotage Your Goals ............ 133

     Tool #10 Find Your Goal Buddy ............ 140

     Tool #11 Feed Forward, Not Backward ............ 146

Chapter 13: **INCENTIVES** ............ 151

     Tool #12 Help Them Invent It ............ 153

     Tool #13 What's It Worth to Them? ............ 159

     Tool #14 Know What Your MVP Values ............ 164

*Chapter 14:* **RECRUIT** ............ 169

     Tool #15 Hire Your Weakness ............ 170

     Tool #16 Stop Networking ............ 176

     Tool #17 Get Someone Ready ............ 181

     Tool #18 Don't Play the Blame Game ............ 187

*Chapter 15:* **EXCITE** ............ 193

     Tool #19 Be Different ............ 194

     Tool #20 Get Heard ............ 200

     Tool #21 What's Your Story? ............ 207

Epilogue ............ 214

Appendix: The Research ............ 217

About the Authors ............ 233

# Foreword

## You Deserve to Be Valued, Respected, and Admired for What Matters

By Frances Hesselbein and Marshall Goldsmith

How proud would you be if your organization won the top spot among *Fortune Magazine's* "Most Admired Companies" or "Best Companies to Work For?" What if Jim Collins rated you a "Level 5 leader," and Gallup ranked your colleagues among "America's Most Admired People?" What if every single person in your organization knew what it took to become J.D. Power Customer Service Champions? Impossible?

We think you have that potential for greatness within you, and so do our friends Mark Thompson and Bonita Buell-Thompson. Drawing on their three decades of corporate leadership experience, in this book they reveal new research that will help you become more valued, respected and admired—not in a superficial way or just for its own sake—but for what matters to you most.

The results of their national study may astonish you. With their colleagues at Stanford and Northwestern, the authors conducted a statistically representative survey of more than 1,000 Americans that asked (as did *Gallup* and *Fortune*), who do you most admire? But then Mark and Bonita took another step to explore something much more significant to your personal and professional success: They discovered the 27 traits Americans most admire in the best leaders and companies, and even more important—*which traits are most essential and why.*

Then they compared the traits most admired in companies and leaders with what participants would most like to be appreciated for as an individual. You may be surprised to see how many of these traits you already have (or are well within your reach) that will enable you personally (and your organization) to become even more respected and admired.

## The Most Valuable People in Your Life and Work

Have you ever felt undervalued at work or home? Who hasn't! Most of us have a deep desire to be valued more by what the authors call, the *Most Valuable People* in our lives—our boss, colleagues, customers, family, and friends. But according to Mark and Bonita's research, very few of us have taken the steps to learn what the important people in our lives actually value. It's painfully ironic to expect to be valued by these MVPs if we don't know what *they* value first! In this book, you'll learn more about how to do that.

Does your team ever underperform or have you lost your mojo to do the work? If so, you're not alone. Gallup found that 67% of people hate their job or feel disengaged. Curious to know why, the authors asked participants in their national survey what percentage of time they invested in their goals and how much did they spend doing meaningful things. The results were downright disturbing: Most people do not see any connection between their daily and long-term goals and what's meaningful to them! It's no surprise that mission statements are ignored, New Year's resolutions languish, and our diets are doomed from the start. We have no hope of achieving our goals, if we don't connect our passions with the objectives in front of us.

The good news is that Mark and Bonita clarify what you can do about it. Your level of engagement and enjoyment are directly related to whether or not you feel your goals are meaningful. And your value to all the MVPs in your life is directly proportionate to what you seek to know about their values and how hard you work to help them achieve it. You will succeed (and be admired) by making sure you support your MVPs in achieving success and admiration for what matters.

In fact, this is an important distinction: You are happiest and most motivated when the admiration you seek is for *something that matters.* What's inspiring about many gifted leaders is that they've suffered long periods in which they were not valued or admired; great people are often misunderstood, even resented or ridiculed. Eventually they persist only because they worked for something meaningful, and that's what helped them reach their greater potential.

What this means for you is that, when you're trying to motivate others to help you, you have to be very clear about what you value and recruit people for your team who love what you're doing, and who are willing to develop the skills to do it so well that they become excellent. If you don't, that same team could be among the two thirds of the population who find work pointless.

If you aspire to become more valued in your work and you'd like to get ahead in your job, Mark and Bonita have a great prescription for you. They'll give you some powerful ways to stop the complaining about why you don't feel appreciated or understood by your MVPs. In this book you will get the tools you need to determine what your MVPs actually value—to stand in their shoes—and keep supporting them until you help them get the message.

When you find a way to give your MVPs the support to achieve their goals in a meaningful way, then they'll reward and admire you. That's the key to success in reaching the top of any "most admired" list, at the office or at home. But more important, that's the secret to finding meaning and happiness in your life and work.

*Frances Hesselbein* is the recipient of the Presidential Medal of Freedom (America's highest civilian honor) and CEO and President of the Hesselbein Institute (formerly Leader to Leader Institute and Peter F. Drucker Foundation for Nonprofit Management)

*Marshall Goldsmith* is a New York Times bestselling author and the #1 Leadership Thinker in the World (according to the Thinker's 50 Conference sponsored by Harvard Business Review)

# Acknowledgements

"Writing a book is an adventure. To begin with, it is a toy and an amusement; then it becomes a mistress, and then it becomes a master, and then a tyrant. The last phase is that just as you are about to be reconciled to your servitude, you kill the monster, and fling him out to the public." —Winston Churchill

The Leader to Leader Institute or Peter F. Drucker Foundation for Nonprofit Management has recently been renamed the Frances Hesselbein Institute, recognizing what Drucker's cofounder, Frances, has continued to contribute to the field of leadership all over the world. Both of us have been honored to serve on the Board of Governors with our mentor, Marshall Goldsmith, and so many other great friends over the years, and want to thank everyone at the Institute for their support on this project.

We are grateful for this collaboration with Adrienne Schultz, whose leadership and insights inspired us, and whose expert writing and editing talents transformed this manuscript. Congratulations to Karen Kreiger at Evolve Publishing—we admire how you're reinventing the spirit and the possibilities for the future of your industry. Bill Chiaravalle, you made this book professional and beautiful at the same time. We give special thanks to Kevin Small, our agent and advisor, whose extraordinary experience and guidance put this book in the hands of tens of thousands of people who matter most.

Rebekkah Dilts has been on our home team committed to helping us do more and be more than we ever thought possible! Joanne Watkins, you keep our world humming no matter where we are on the planet.

Professor Kelly Goldsmith and Lauren Cheatham at the Kellogg School of Management at Northwestern University and Professor Cliff Nass at Stanford University have mentored us as we reviewed research methodologies, encouraging us to find bold new ways to think about how America values leadership. Lauren, as you depart Northwestern for the next chapter in your career at Stanford, we want to thank you for the patient, 24/7 guidance you given us, and sound analysis of the data.

We have had the privilege of learning from and working with Sir Richard Branson; Jean Oelwang, CEO; Andrew Purvis, COO; and their brilliant teams in London and New York, along with Jon Peachey, CEO of Virgin Management USA. You are leading a world-changing movement to Screw Business As Usual, and we're proud to be a part of it.

Our thanks to Ed Reilly, CEO of the American Management Association, Joan Synder, Amazon founder Jeff Bezos, Maya Angelou, Nelson Mandela, YouTube founder Chad Hurley, Jane Tewson, Ben Cohen of Ben & Jerry's, CEO of HSM/World Business Forum Pat Meier, Four Seasons' Alex von Bidder, Charles "Chuck" Schwab, Tony Robbins, XPrize Founder Peter Diamandis, Success Magazine's Darren Hardy, HARO founder Peter Shankman, John Hagel, Michael and Sydney Cresci, Jim Kwik, Mandalay Entertainment CEO Peter Guber, Mark Victor Hansen, Jack Canfield, Marci Shimoff, Joe Polish, Rick Smolan, Greg Link, Stephen Covey, Larry Benet, Randy Williams at Keiretsu Forum, Ixia CEO Atul Bhatnagar, Chris Fralic, Smule founders Jeff Smith and Ge Wang, ABC News' Teri Whitcraft and CBS News' Brian Banmiller, John F. Kennedy University President Steve Stargardter and Entrepreneurship Institute Founder Raul Deju.

We're proud to have friends to support us like Jack and Cherry Jia, Dr. Daveed Frazier, Dr. Rekha Parameswaran, Keith Ferrazzi, Jordan

Roberts, Dr. Annette Ermshar and Dan Monahan, Dr. Martha Reitman, Peter Sims, Pip Coburn, Sunny Bates, TED/Ink CEO Lakshmi Pratury, Reid Hoffman, Bill Gates, Barrett Cordero, Beverly Tracey, Ed Primeau, Karen Harris, Jason Jennings, Tim Sanders, John Maxwell, Michelle and Chris McCormick, Jeanette and Roger Hajjar, Steve and Sharon Teeter, Daria and Eric Waggoner, Julie and Pat Belanger, Julie Woods-Moss, Ivy Ross, Lori and Doug Becker; Brad, Marjorie, Fritz and Lisa Buell—our cherished family whose love keeps us going!

When we think of "America's Most Admired," there's no one who deserves to be more valued than you.

**—Mark Thompson and Bonita Buell-Thompson**

# SECTION 1

# What You Want

# 1

## Are You Valued?

Our commuter jet was rolling out on the runway on Southwest flight number 49 just before dawn when there was a brief flash of lightning and a heavy downpour. The flight attendant began the same old safety talk that nearly all the passengers could by now repeat from memory. But none of us could imagine what would happen next. Half the cabin was reading and the other half was already fast sleep at that hour. As we neared takeoff, the flight attendant was becoming increasingly annoyed at our total lack of interest in her lecture on how to fasten seatbelts. She suddenly shouted into the microphone.

## ADMIRED

"Listen up!" she demanded, swinging the seatbelt in the air. "You think you're experts on this sort of thing, but if this plane falls out of the sky during this storm, I guarantee you're not going to be napping, reading your Kindle, or chatting with your pals." We couldn't quite believe what we were hearing. "If we get into trouble up there, you're going to be thinking about how you might have had a tiny chance at survival if you had listened to me! Then you'll think about your loved ones and see your life pass before your eyes as we fall out of the sky."

I dropped my iPad, which was supposed to be turned off by now anyway. Every last person in the cabin was now riveted, giving her our rapt attention, and wishing we had missed this flight.

"Okay, here's what's going to happen," she continued breathlessly. "If there is a sudden crisis and a change in cabin pressure, these oxygen masks will pop out of the ceiling." She whipped the canary yellow device from her pocket and hung it over my head like a noose. "Don't just sit there waiting to be saved. This is your big chance! Take action! Grab the mask. Put it on yourself first, then put it on your child. And if you have more than one child," she said smiling, "you might want to consider which one has the *most potential!*"

## Becoming Essential

The cabin burst into laughter, everyone relieved by the punch line. But the flight attendant's dark humor stuck with me for the rest of the bumpy ride. It occurred to me that emergencies are not the only times we are forced to make hard decisions. The punch line of her morbid joke was also a brutal metaphor for the tough choices leaders make when resources are scarce and competition is fierce.

## ARE YOU VALUED?

Your boss is constantly evaluating whom he values most—who will get the oxygen and opportunities. Companies are making sacrifices every day. Leaders can no longer afford to support a project just because the people working on it have great intentions. It has to demonstrate extraordinary value, rapid progress, and high return on effort or ROI. Your customers are making the same trade-offs about what to buy and what to ignore based on what *they* value—not necessarily what *you* love about your product or services—and they'll give you less time than ever to impress them.

> If you want to become essential, you must both make sure you're delivering value to your MVPs and that they recognize that value.

You may deserve to be valued, respected, and admired for what you do, but your customers, your boss, and everyone else you know has a growing list of obligations and distractions competing for their time and attention. How do you break through the noise?

The answer is to better understand what drives value for your best customers, your boss, and your loved ones. These are your *Most Valuable People or MVPs*—those who make the biggest, most meaningful impact on your work and life. If you want to become essential, you must both make sure you're delivering value to your MVPs and that they *recognize* that value.

When your boss decides whom or what deserves her attention, she is choosing among dozens of worthy candidates, and she is basing her choice on your *perceived* value to her. You won't be essential to her until you can demonstrate a deeper understanding of how she defines success, and how you're helping her achieve her immediate needs and

ADMIRED

future goals.

## Finding Value for Ourselves

Our passion for this concept of being valued began for both of us while we were kids in school, a time when we feared we had no potential. Both of us struggled with the symptoms of dyslexia—learning issues that impacted our sense of self-worth. And our parents already had their hands full. Both families, on too many occasions to count, wondered where their next meal or next mortgage payment would come from. At the time, none of us felt valued for our potential contribution.

Then we both dealt with personal tragedies that changed our lives forever. Bonita's older brother, David—a brilliant young man who was already contributing to the world of science—died of cancer at age 21. Mark's brother, Bob Jr., despite his doctor's best efforts, didn't get the oxygen he needed at birth. The brain damage was permanent. Both families saw their faith shaken and their resources stretched to the limit by those difficult circumstances. For as long as we can remember, we have been incredulous that two such valuable lives ended before our brothers could even begin to realize their potential.

These events inspired what would become our mission in life: To help people and their organizations realize their greatest potential *value*. To discover what makes people valuable, respected, and admired, we have conducted global and national surveys, and engaged with hundreds of the world's most successful people face-to-face, from Nelson Mandela and Richard Branson, to Steve Jobs and the Dalai Lama. We met with the presidents of nations, Nobel laureates, Olympians, Academy Award winners, more than 20 billionaires, and community servants without financial resources who are having great impact far from the public spotlight.

## ARE YOU VALUED?

Through this work, we've seen major trends emerge and have developed tools for people to make success more sustainable, including a "game" they can play to uncover their deeper values and unlock various possibilities and opportunities that will help you create a strategy for your future success.

In this book, we will share many of the lessons we've learned from our research and from our experiences playing the game with high achievers. One of the most important things we've discovered is that the best upside opportunities come along when you partner with and invest in talented people and organizations that are undervalued. As executive coaches who are also venture capitalists, we bet our heart, soul, and life savings on helping winners whose potential isn't fully valued in the market and who deserve greater respect from those who matter most.

We believe that you deserve to be valued and admired for what matters. And in this book, we'll show you how to do that. In the first two sections, we'll provide a roadmap to both clarifying what you value most and understanding what your MVPs value. This will help you create a powerful bridge between what they need from you and what you can sustainably offer. Then we'll provide six fundamental strategies—using the word A.D.M.I.R.E. as the acronym—each of which offer tools to help you cut through the clutter and double your value to the people who matter most.

Let's get started!

22

# 2

## How to Become an MVP

We've all felt undervalued at some point in our lives and we'd love to have our boss, customers, and family appreciate us for the many things we do for them. To be more valued, respected and admired, you must know what the important people in your professional and personal life—your Most Valuable People or MVPs—value most. Do you know what your MVPs care about? Are you sure you're giving them exactly what *they* value, not just what *you* value? It has to be both.

## First, Give Value

The most admired people are those who focus on giving more value than they expect from others in every interaction. Reciprocity is the first step to being more valued. It would be fabulous if your MVPs value what you care about as much as you do, but it's rarely that simple.

Whether you're running a household or managing a multinational corporation, you may feel you're already generous with the MVPs in your life. You've always had the best of intentions and, after all this time, you deserve their applause for all that you do for them. But it can't be all about you until it's *also* all about them. Some call this *Servant Leadership*.

> Are you giving your MVPs exactly what they value, not just what you value? It has to be both.

Being valued by others is about finding the intersection between what you can and want to contribute and what your MVPs need. As with the oxygen mask that drops from the ceiling of an airplane in distress, we must take care of our own needs before we can help others. Everyone, including your MVPs, has their own agenda. Not only is it essential to be clear about your needs and goals, if you want to serve your MVPs better and be more admired in return, you must help them achieve what is important to them at work and in life.

## Do You Feel Valued?

*Somewhat.* Perhaps not as much as you should. With the help of our friends at Stanford and Northwestern Universities, we asked more than 1,000 Americans in a national survey to rate how valued they feel, with 1 being the least valued and 7, the most. Our respondents gave their boss or customers a 4—they felt moderately valued by these MVPs. Good, but not great.

They thought their families appreciated them a bit more. The respondents gave them a rating of 5 on average; and many said their families valued them a 6 out of 7. That's pretty darn good.

## Do You Know What Your MVPs Value?

*Nope. Not really.* When we asked our survey participants whether they knew what their boss or customers valued, they gave themselves a miserly score of 2 on a scale of 7. Even for their families, they rated themselves only a 3 when asked how well they knew what their loved ones valued. Yikes! In face-to-face seminars, we also found a similar disconnect between people's desire to be valued and their knowledge of what others desire. Our students were able to tell us instantly whether or not they were sufficiently valued by others. Rarely did anyone ever say they were overvalued. But when asked what their MVPs valued, we were surprised how often we got a blank stare.

Despite all the news on the importance of *knowing your customer*, very few people do it enough at work or in life. Reciprocity takes enormous effort. The irony is that even though it rarely crosses our minds to consider what our boss, clients, or family members really value, we're insulted when our MVPs don't value *us*!

There is a good reason for this. It's easy to imagine what *we think* others value in us. We know a lot about what we have to offer. We know what we were asked to do in our job, for example, but focus very little on how or whether the recipients of that work—our bosses, colleagues, and customers—value it. But in business and life, success is in knowing (and

**ADMIRED**

then doing) what the customer wants and needs, not what we think they should want and need.

## What Are Your MVPs Looking for in a Leader?

One of the major reasons you may be undervalued as a leader is because there is a big difference between how you want to be admired as a person and what others are looking for in their leaders. In our national survey, we asked what traits participants admire in a leader, and then compared those traits with what they wanted to be admired for as a person. Turns out that they aren't the same thing.

The top five or six traits are similar for both questions. People said they both want to be admired for and want leaders who are:

- *Smart*
- *Caring*
- *Hard-working*
- *Dependable*
- *Honest*
- *Competent*

Put those traits on your checklist as the leadership behaviors that are always appreciated and admired. In 30 years of research on leadership, these traits are the most frequently cited. But similarity ends there.

The big difference between what we want to be valued for and what we say we value in our leaders emerged when we asked participants about the rest of the most admired characteristics. In addition to these five or six universal traits, they said they want their leaders also to be *visionary, inspiring, cause-driven/moral, determined, and courageous.* For themselves, the list was different. The top ten traits they want to be admired for also include being *creative/imaginative, supportive, loyal, fun loving, and friendly.*

## HOW TO BECOME AN MVP

These are all good traits, and we found 27 in all. It's impossible for most of us to embody all of them at once, of course. So we took this inquiry another important step further than other research on the topic. We asked participants how engaged they are with work, how enjoyable it is, and how much of it is meaningful. There's tons of proof that people who love their work and think it matters actually do more, do it better, and are great to be around. For *only* those people who felt engaged in meaningful and enjoyable work, they wanted these characteristic in their leaders—several traits had not made the top ten in other sample sizes. Highly motivated people said they want their leaders to be:

- *Supportive/Helpful*
- *Straightforward/Clear*
- *Hardworking/ Ambitious*
- *Cooperative*

- *Honest*
- *Loyal*
- *Fun-loving/Friendly*
- *Family Focused*

Those are eight traits well worth aspiring for. What this means is that if you want to become more valued and admired for what you do for your MVPs, you need to focus on how you're exhibiting these key characteristics. How are you demonstrating to your customers, coworkers, and boss that you're *supportive*? Are you making sure that what you say and do is *straightforward and clear*? Think about how your actions and behaviors represent you for all eight traits.

In order to be admired as a leader you need to prioritize the eight hot button traits that motivate MVPs value most. We call these your *Portfolio of Priorities*, and we'll review these in the next chapter.

## Find a Place to Call Home

If you want to feel more valued, then you need to find a community of people who share those values. What we mean by environment is a place or ecosystem where people are actively involved in your profession, share your values, and where you can make yourself known and valuable.

If you want to fly, hang out with people who do that. We have a dear friend who could not rest until he became a fighter pilot. Pat Belanger became a Top Gun because he loved the discipline, duty, and outrageous action as an airman, and the sense of service and contribution it gave him. By pursuing that dream with excellence and passion, he is today admired by that tribe.

We have another pal, Dr. Daveed Frazier, whose first love is spine surgery, but like me (Mark), also has a passion for producing Broadway shows. In addition to our other responsibilities, we can't expect to be successful with theatre productions unless we invest time in building relationships locally in the New York theater community. If you want to participate in a field or endeavor where you want to be valued and make an admirable contribution, you have to show up and serve in ways that are valued in that business or in that neighborhood. That's how you eventually become an MVP. Make it your mission to find the right place where people gather who are engaged in your passion and where you can increase your chances to seize the right opportunities and meet the right influencers.

# 3

## Create Your Portfolio of Priorities

**It is likely no surprise that a few hot issues drive your Most Valuable People's behavior.** But what may appear to be idiosyncrasies (that may delight or annoy you) are much more important than that. In fact understanding them is crucial to delivering value, and we call them your MVPs' *Portfolio of Priorities*. To identify them you have to shift from focusing entirely on what you're selling to what your MVPs really want or need to buy. Help them to be successful in ways *that they notice*. How can you provide oxygen to those burning ambitions of theirs?

If you want your boss to value you and your work, then it's easy to start by delivering what you promised. And that might be enough. But to stand out, it's essential to take another step. You must find out what will make your boss successful with *her* boss, and what her ambitions may be for her life.

Margaret, a personal trainer, found out the hard way that her boss is obsessed with improving how quickly and effectively his team responds to customers. Though he had never explained this priority to her, he expected every phone call and email to be answered instantly. And so when Margaret didn't respond to his email for three days, he wasn't a happy camper.

Margaret was focused on working with customers out on the floor, and they loved her, but she wasn't attentive to email. Margaret quickly got the message that responsiveness was important to her boss and she needed to find a way to do that while showing him how well she was keeping up with their MVPs.

The first step was to agree on his portfolio of priorities. Responding to customers immediately was obviously number one, but helping customers at the gym was a close second. They agreed to get Margaret a smartphone so that her boss could reach her with urgent matters and she could send non-urgent calls to voicemail when she was busy helping customers.

## Be Honest if You Don't Agree

When you and your MVP agree to a set of priorities, you both must be honest in your willingness to uphold it. Because your MVPs will pay close attention to the things that matter most to them, they'll know immediately if you're just going through the motions and not making a real effort to deliver on their biggest needs. For Margaret, email was marginally important. Because it was at the top of her boss's portfolio of priorities (even though he didn't do a good job of communicating that at first), she had the opportunity to either delight or disappoint him.

If something is unimportant to you, it's sometimes hard to believe it's important to your MVP. Suspend judgment—not forever, but long enough to see if there is a desire that you both can share (in Margaret's case it was making customers happy). You may ultimately decide you can't come to an understanding and agree to disagree, but take a moment to see if there's some deeper common ground. So many opportunities are lost simply because we see something as trivial that an MVP sees as valuable. If we'd stop judging that difference of opinion, we might find a remarkable overlap in our interests. It's not easy, but it is necessary if you want to be valued by others. It takes time.

## It Takes Time

In our interviews with the greatest achievers, very few people or companies figure out what customers want or value instantly. Instagram defined value so well for Facebook's Mark Zuckerberg, he paid $1billion for it. But the rest of us mortals take years to launch a company, earn a customer or partner's trust, establish a career, produce a play, or learn how to prepare a gourmet meal. The extensive time and effort you invest into finding and creating value rarely reflects the few moments it takes your customer to consume it.

"The customer may never know the level of care you took in knowing what that hungry diner wanted to eat—the attention to every detail of the experience your restaurant delivered," star chef Jamie Oliver told me

# ADMIRED

during an interview in the kitchen of his flagship restaurant, *Fifteen*. "What that means is that you spend a lot of effort learning what people are hoping for or secretly desire long before you start shopping, chopping, and cooking."

> To identify your MVPs' portfolio of priorities, shift from focusing entirely on what you're selling to what they really want or need to buy.

"The idea that you must *know your customer* is bloody obvious," he smiled, "but then we forget to do it all the time in our busy days. We let arrogance, wishful thinking or plain expediency replace what we know about our customers—and then you have the nerve to feel hurt when they don't acknowledge you?"

He sampled a soup for that night's menu and grimaced. "It's important to have your opinion. But you don't deserve to be admired until you prove to the people you're serving that you care about how *they think* it should taste—and they can feel your love in every meal."

CREATE YOUR PORTFOLIO OF PRIORITIES

# Putting It to Work for You

This is a list of questions you can use to get to know your MVP better and identify their Portfolio of Priorities. Answer these questions for each key person in your life (your customer, boss, spouse, friend, or yourself) with whom you want to build a relationship.

1.  Who does your MVP admire and what characteristics do they admire in those other people?

..........................................................................................................................

..........................................................................................................................

..........................................................................................................................

..........................................................................................................................

..........................................................................................................................

2.  What are the key roles your MVP plays? (for example, CEO, father, spouse, friend, daughter, skier, board member, volunteer, neighbor) In each of these roles, what objectives do they have?

..........................................................................................................................

..........................................................................................................................

..........................................................................................................................

..........................................................................................................................

..........................................................................................................................

**ADMIRED**

3. For each role, what do they love most?

........................................................................................................

........................................................................................................

........................................................................................................

........................................................................................................

........................................................................................................

4. What do they complaint about? What does that tell you about what they value?

........................................................................................................

........................................................................................................

........................................................................................................

........................................................................................................

........................................................................................................

What hobbies or interests do they have?

........................................................................................................

........................................................................................................

........................................................................................................

........................................................................................................

........................................................................................................

## CREATE YOUR PORTFOLIO OF PRIORITIES

5. What are they good at? What expertise or abilities do they have?

6. How could you help them get more of what they value?

36

# 4

## Define What Success Means

**Most people can give great detail about the problems they are facing.** But it's a rare person who can be equally detailed about what they consider success—whether it's success in their next job, next staff meeting, or even their next email. Before you can become better valued by your MVPs, you must get clear about your definition of success so that you can create a roadmap to accomplish it, and then recruit others to help you get there.

After another sleepless night, Kelly reluctantly approached the room for her divorce proceeding. She couldn't stomach another contentious "I'm

**ADMIRED**

right; you're wrong" free-for-all. Their bickering was going nowhere, and not she, her ex, or her kids would benefit from all the exhausting effort.

She stopped short of the door and considered an idea that had come and gone throughout the marathon of awful meetings. She hadn't given it much thought until now, and she leaned against the wall and sighed. It was worth a try. So Kelly forced herself to take a few moments to imagine the impossible: What would a successful divorce meeting look like. She got clear about what she needed— happy children, basic resources, and the freedom to make a fresh start in her life.

> When you clearly define success at the very beginning, both parties are more likely work toward the same goal.

As the meeting began, she asked her ex what would make for a successful session, in his eyes. He was stunned for a moment, and his attorney smirked. But then he saw exactly where she was headed with this. The impasse was broken and as the meeting progressed, with their shared definition of success clearly in mind, Kelly was able to find win-win situations (and agree to some palatable compromises) for the first time. Every time the discussion descended into name-calling and accusations, she could remind everyone of their goal and refocus the discourse to get them closer toward that vision. This kept the meeting on track and less emotional.

## You Don't Have to Be "Right" to Be Effective

It is surprising to discover how different each our definitions of success

## DEFINE WHAT SUCCESS MEANS

can be. And too often we move forward assuming we know what success looks like for our MVPs when in fact we are projecting our values onto others, blocking our ability to actually hear the other person. Just like Kelly and her ex, we frequently spend our time in meetings talking more than we listen and wondering why the person across the table doesn't agree with us. When we clearly define success at the very beginning, both parties are more likely work toward the same goal. Take a few minutes to find out what everyone wants to take away from the meeting so you can make it productive and rewarding.

In our seminars at major companies and universities, we're always impressed to see how people use this technique in dozens of different fields, professions, and industries. A public health official used this defining success tool in a meeting to get people less focused on their personal agenda and more focused on the customer. Everyone agreed that a healthy community was their shared definition of success. If anyone strayed from that larger objective, the health official could remind everyone they had agreed to the definition at the beginning of the meeting. When the going gets tough, the cause you are working toward is more important than any individual's current mood.

Another executive in our class had made a short-term loan to a family member. After many months passed without any mention of reimbursement, she knew she needed to confront her loved one. But before asking for her money back, she asked for her family member's definition of success. Understanding this let the women make her case that paying her back would bring a greater feeling of success to this family member and avoided a "you owe me" discussion.

For a client who managed a fulfillment unit, defining success helped his team determine whose packages would get done first. The fulfillment team suddenly was more aware of how their role influenced customer relationships. By having them define success to prioritize the fulfillment

**ADMIRED**

of the orders, the team saw how important their role was in the success of the firm. So defining success in this fulfillment department gave them a greater sense of purpose.

## Winning Over Your MVPs

For the past 30 years we've been fascinated by how different people are when it comes to their definition of success. For our book, *Success Built to Last*—the sequel to the business class, *Built to Last*—we partnered with Wharton School of Business to conduct a World Success Survey of high achievers. We focused on working professionals in more than 110 nations. The results showed that successful people define success in at least three distinctly different ways, and that by defining it for yourself and others early and often, you can greatly improve your odds and make your success more sustainable.

Before embarking on any new goal or mission, use these three definitions of success to check in with yourself on what matters most. In fact, you'll win the support of anyone important to you—your MVPs will feel heard and understood—if you can find out the "three Ps".

*1) Purpose:* What impact does she really want to have? How does she want to make a difference?

*2) Passions:* What personal interests or talents could she apply to this project (she'll have more fun, be more engaged and resilient to setbacks if this is personal).

*3) Performance:* How will she measure short-term success today in this meeting and every step along the timeline of your project?

You may have short-term success by applying a lot of effort to any one of these three definitions, but professionals who sustained their success

## DEFINE WHAT SUCCESS MEANS

for 20 years or more always focused on finding the intersection of all three of these definitions for themselves *and* people who matter to them.

# Putting It to Work for You

This is a worksheet for your top priorities to help you define success for those objectives. Complete these questions for each of your top objectives.

1.  What is the purpose of this priority or objective?

........................................................................................................

........................................................................................................

........................................................................................................

........................................................................................................

........................................................................................................

2.  How will you measure success personally? What end result do you want?

........................................................................................................

........................................................................................................

........................................................................................................

........................................................................................................

**ADMIRED**

3. Who else is defining success for this priority?

........................................................................................................

........................................................................................................

........................................................................................................

........................................................................................................

........................................................................................................

4. How will others evaluate whether you've achieved success?

........................................................................................................

........................................................................................................

........................................................................................................

........................................................................................................

........................................................................................................

5. What are the different measurements for success?

........................................................................................................

........................................................................................................

........................................................................................................

........................................................................................................

........................................................................................................

## DEFINE WHAT SUCCESS MEANS

6. What impact will success have on each stakeholder group?

7. What's in the way of success?

44

# 5

## The Law of Distraction

Have you ever felt overwhelmed by the blizzard of conflicting priorities at home and at the office? *Who hasn't!* You can be certain that your MVPs are suffering too. That's the number one complaint of the world's most successful people we interviewed. As humans we have a primal need to be creatively engaged—to be up to something that will result in some meaningful impact. If only those dreams didn't generate so much spam.

**ADMIRED**

The problem is that it's easier today than ever to waste time. We live within a perfect storm of attractive distractions—emails, cell phones, texting, games, and media—that provide instant gratification or satisfy urgent matters. Not that there's anything wrong with that—except that it's hard to have impact or feel you've accomplished anything tangible after spending the day responding to small requests at work, posting on Facebook and Twitter, and keeping up with the Kardashians.

## You Can Have It All, But Not All at Once

Of course, all of us have been feeling "the overwhelm" since long before the dawn of the Internet (which by the way was supposed to give us tools to reduce the clutter in our lives). In the 80's classic, *Seven Habits of Highly Effective People*, Stephen Covey cautions us against compiling massive to-do lists without first taking a serious reality check: "Cut your priorities down to a few good things that matter most," he insisted. "You can have it all, but not all at once!" Covey led a revolution in day planners and getting organized, and his work is still our mantra. Your life will be transformed if you have the self-discipline and attention span to take his sage advice.

In a rare opportunity, Covey invited Mark and Bonita to his beautiful French Provincial-style home overlooking Provo, Utah. He and his two sons talked with us privately about how to manage stress in the new millennium—with the unusual perspective that comes from sitting in the Zen-like setting of the his backyard terrace.

What was the most critical habit that touched Covey personally after 30 years of teaching this stuff? It was "the foundation habit—being proactive—upon which all the other habits are based," he mused. Covey said there is a big difference between giving your attention only to

## THE LAW OF DISTRACTION

urgent matters that compete for your mindshare and the more important things that will help you prosper in the long term. Our primal brain is easily seduced by fight-or-flight urges, which means that anything that feels remotely like a crisis—and does not require deep thought—will be given priority. Covey believes that's backwards. Unless you're being chased by a saber-tooth tiger, it's likely that you will benefit from stopping to distinguish between "fire drills" and other issues that would have a longer term impact on your work. In other words, you may have to address certain pressing matters in the next hour, but think about what you need to do this week to invest in your long-term work and life objectives and carve out some time for that too.

## The Myth of Multitasking

Many people perceive that multitasking actually works, but research shows it's a disaster if you really want to accomplish anything meaningful. Stanford Professor Cliff Nass tested college students at one of the world's best universities, where many of the greatest technology breakthroughs were conceived; so you could safely assume these young folks might be at the top of their class when it came to using multitasking tools.

> **Stanford research has found multitasking severely limits memory, accuracy, and productivity in performing tasks**

The surprise was that even here at Stanford he found multitasking severely limited participants' memory, accuracy, and productivity in performing tasks compared with students who did one thing at a time. In fact, their concentration was

**ADMIRED**

damaged by multitasking. They lost their ability to focus on any one relevant issue, and didn't perform nearly as well as people who kept their eye on one meaningful outcome at a time.

In another study with *Discovery Magazine*, Nass tested teenage girls who immersed themselves in social media. He found that they had lower self-esteem and lost their ability to socialize happily or effectively in real situations. The girls may have intended to have fun and connect with friends, but over time engaging in social media actually inhibited their ability to read human faces and get along with others in person.

## From Entertainment to Addiction

You could argue that much of the online media we consume is harmless entertainment. However, Nielsen reports that U.S. monthly time spent on social networks and blogs topped a billion hours, with another half a billion hours spent on online games. Americans spend 15 million hours a month on entertainment news sites alone—almost half of that at the office. And each week the average American consumes about 40 hours of combined TV and online content—that's a full-time job!

Granted there is a huge range of good and bad content, but by investing too much time in visual media you run the risk of ingesting lots of empty calories. Does it get us any closer to creating value or having a meaningful impact on our lives or others'? All to often, it doesn't.

It's supposed to be entertainment, but the huge quantity of time we spend on these pursuits sounds more like an addiction. For too many people, media consumption is being used like a drug to medicate our sense of isolation and lack of purpose. The irony of any addiction is not that it makes us feel bad in the moment, but that it seductively makes us feel good without providing any lasting value.

## Stop Vicarious Living—The Law of Distraction

Television, movies, internet surfing, critiquing others, or comparing yourself to everyone else—that's all *vicarious living*, as our friend and leadership guru Marshall Goldsmith calls it. While it may feel creative temporarily to analyze a supermodel's latest publicity, unless you're a reporter for a tabloid, spending too much time doing this means you aren't investing precious time in reaching your own goals. You're just living somebody else's life—not yours. There isn't anything wrong with watching television with the goal of relaxing, but when you go from show to show without any goal in mind – are you sure that's the life you want?

## Ten Steps to Focus

There's something deeper happening too. Media studies indicate that people develop a sense of affiliation with celebrities they don't know because they spend so much time reading, thinking, and talking about them. The proverbial six degrees of separation that you may be hoping to find between you and Kevin Bacon is an urban myth. (Sadly, studies now show that the six degrees experiment was wishful thinking, not research, and was flawed in the first place.)

No matter how interesting Kevin's life may seem to be, he won't commit to help you meet your goals and objectives. But you know plenty of people who can and will help you if you can train yourself to focus more on positive interactions than on mind-numbing and time-wasting ones. Here are 10 key steps to help manage the overwhelm:

1.  ***Set three priorities for the day.*** If we did all the things that self-help books told us we should do, we would need a 400-hour week.

# ADMIRED

Choose three top objectives for the next 24 hours and try to meet them.

2. ***Do what matters most, first.*** Our world is filled with opportunity and there are a lot of great things we "should" do, but the most important are those that matter to you. What are the essential activities that will further your meaningful goals? Whittle down your to-do list to include only the things you care most about. Then do these things before you open your inbox or begin other day-to-day matters.

3. ***Make some temporary sacrifices.*** The difficult thing is that, naturally, you care about more than just one thing. Simplify as best you can, but don't add to the list without taking something else off. I love a few TV shows but that doesn't put food on the table or keep me in shape. How about prerecording those favorite programs and using them as a reward while you walk on the treadmill? Remember, you can have it all; just not all at once.

4. ***Don't get it all done.*** We have a dear friend and colleague who manages a large professional organization at Stanford. She's a physician and has a husband and three fabulous kids; she travels internationally quarterly and finds time for knitting, dinner parties with high achievers, and is working toward her black belt in karate.

5. When I asked Martha how she gets it all done she smiled. "I don't. I have to select the actions that are going to give me the most return today." She is a skilled and passionate cook, but sets an appointment to do that on special occasions and doesn't try to cook every day. "For example, I don't chop onions; I buy them prepared. My family pitches in and learns valuable skills in the process. And I focus on what matters to me and I accomplish that."

# THE LAW OF DISTRACTION

6. *It's Okay to Fire a Friend.* We make the best choices in friends when we base our selection on how well they support who we are. Remember that you do pick your friends and you can fire the ones who drain your energy without giving anything back. Instead surround yourself with friends who help you find joy, meaning, and growth—those who help you be who you are and who you want to be. If you see yourself as a businesswoman who has a family, seek friends who support you in running your career. If you are a family man with a full-time job, your friends will more likely support your family role.

7. In his bestselling book our friend Keith Ferrazzi wisely advises you to *Never Eat Alone*—always plan a meal with someone who matters. Keith advises that you recruit a Lifeline group, much as Napoleon Hill encouraged us to create Mastermind groups, which have grown all over the U.S. These are groups of caring mentors who support you and each other—people who've got your back. Who are the key people who can help you make a difference? Get time with them on your calendar.

8. *Streamline daily and weekly activities:* Tasks that take ten minutes a day every day add up to a little over a work week every year. If you can streamline these routine tasks, you can gain a lot of time for doing tasks that really matter to you. Checklists, convenient workspaces, and automation are great ways to streamline routine tasks.

9. *Delegate:* Find a person who loves a task you dislike. As a VC, Mark loves financial strategy but he hates accounting, so we treasure the woman who we found to lead our accounting. Search for ways to automate, eliminate, or double up on several tasks. Can you use Internet services to do errands for you? (Buy it on Amazon) Are

**ADMIRED**

there services in your area that pick up and drop off dry cleaning so you can focus on what matters?

10. *Sharpen your skills.* Wait a minute, we're talking about streamlining work, and you've just added a training class? Our national survey showed that what Americans most admire in leaders, companies, and each other is *competence.* As our coauthor and mentor, Brian Tracy always advises: What one new skill could change your life the most? Become more proficient at that. Set aside time to learn a new skill.

11. *Reduce interruptions.* Every time you stop a task and come back to it later you lose 5 to 15 minutes. It takes us a while to figure out what we were doing. This is also the number one reason we make mistakes. Find blocks of time when you can execute tasks start to finish and establish ways to minimize interruptions while you work. When poet and author Maya Angelou wanted to be left alone to write, she rented a hotel room and told the staff that she didn't want anyone to refresh towels or turn down the bed.

12. *Have a place to stash stuff that doesn't matter.* America's closets, garages and ministorage companies are bursting at the seams, and maybe that's not a bad thing. I (Mark) have a hard time throwing out things that don't relate to my current goals because I worry they might support a future passion. Have a place to stash these things you're not currently using so you can get to them if and when you need them.

# 6

## The Passion Trap

**Long before you reach puberty, your parents are more likely to be afraid of your passions than delighted by them.** When you're small, they have good reason to fear your strong desire to climb stairs, tall chairs, and bookshelves. And when you get a little older they try not to worry that you might really become a paleontologist, back-up dancer, or another passion du jour that they believe will not serve your (or their) long-term aspirations. That's usually true in school, too. After all, following *your* passions means you may not follow *their* instructions.

## ADMIRED

We're encouraged to follow our passions as long as they don't put at risk any of the plans other people have for us. That leads to what we call the *Passion Trap*, following the dreams of others instead of our own. If you don't protect and nurture them, your passions can easily be trampled by MVPs who feel differently (and sometimes strongly) about what projects, careers, or people are best for you.

> If you continue to do what the powerful people in your life want you to do at the expense of pursuing your dreams, you will never achieve your highest potential.

Following your passions can be more difficult than you realize. You may feel they distract you from your immediate objectives or obligations you've made. And passions aren't always politically correct or organized (unless your passion is for organization or politics, then they're amazingly effortless, irresistible, and make you look like a genius). But Passion is a magic ingredient in all stories of lasting success. In our interviews and research with world leaders we hear the same piece of brutal advice from every billionaire, president, and Nobel laureate: *If your passion conflicts with the people you want to be valued and admired by, find a different group of MVPs, at least for a while.*

Wanting to be admired and valued for something that does not matter to you is a common trap that will make you miserable. Plus many others truly *are* passionate about it and they'll be far more effective than you. If you continue to do whatever the powerful people in your life want you to do at the expense of pursuing your dreams, you will never achieve your highest potential.

THE PASSION TRAP

## How Quincy Jones Discovered His Passion

What if your peers and mentors were gang members and bullies, as they were for Quincy Jones? It would not only disappoint his MVPs to find out he wanted to make a different career choice, it could have been life threatening.

As we sipped Bloody Marys in his home near Hollywood, "Q" as he prefers to be called, shared stories with us about his training with the mafia. The room was jammed with dozens of Grammy's and other awards and photos that remind visitors that Q remains one of the most admired artists in recording history. For more than fifty years he has been involved in the music industry as a musician, composer, and producer working with the likes of Oprah, Will Smith, Ray Charles, Frank Sinatra, Michael Jackson, and countless others. Not only has he discovered many other icons of music—and of the silver screen, as well—he's also been able to draw out a sense of artistic purpose in himself and others. When he identified that mission in his life it was under a very unique set of circumstances.

Born in Chicago, Quincy Jones moved with his family to Bremerton, Washington when he was ten years old. During WWII his father worked at the shipyards and Quincy was left alone for most of the day with his brother and stepbrother. "We were thugs when we were little," he recounts. "We'd go all over town breaking into stores and burning things down, just being idiots at eleven years old." The boys had learned from the best of the mafia in Chicago where their father worked as a master carpenter for some of the most notorious gangsters in town. They grew up seeing piles of money and piles of guns, and a young Quincy aspired to live that lifestyle one day.

That was, until he experienced one special, completely accidental moment during a night of mischief. That night the boys broke into a

**ADMIRED**

recreation center of a military base because they had heard about a late-night delivery of lemon meringue pies and ice cream. After they'd had their fill of pie and used the rest in a food fight, they began to prowl around the building. Quincy broke into the administration room and saw a small spinet piano sitting in the corner. About to close the door, something changed his mind and he went inside.

"I touched the keys and that was it. It changed my life. I knew it inside, too. I knew it would be what I'd do for the rest of my life."

## Don't Fight Your Passion

Passionate people try harder to achieve their goals, and are happier. In the office they're more productive, creative, and innovative—they're even paid more, but they're worth more. Passionate people take fewer sick days and they even live longer.

So here's the warning from Q and everyone we've interviewed over the past 20 years: For every person who is half hearted in their work, there are plenty of people hungry, willing, and able to grab those opportunities. For that reason, you're not safe in that job you think is safe if you don't love it. You're not safe in that safe relationship if you don't love that person. Relationships that are built to last require the kind of resilience that comes only from knowing what matters to you and honoring those feelings with your passion.

Warren Buffett loves what he does everyday and worries about people who pour all of their time and energy into a job that they loath. As you might imagine, almost everyone he meets pitches him business proposals or asks for advice. Buffett once told us that the many talented people who approach him may have a good track record of performance and a sense of who to serve in the marketplace, but they too often

## THE PASSION TRAP

overlook passion. As we said in chapter 4, purpose and performance are two of the three main components of success for the world's highest achievers, but the third P—passion—is equally essential to long-term success. Buffett told me, "People often say they'll grab something they're passionate about in their next job or next promotion. They say they'll get to that later, but putting off passion is a little like saving up sex for your old age. Not a very good idea!"

Buffett isn't the only successful person who followed his passion instead of some other external driver like money, fame, or approval. And for that reason, he's widely admired for something that matters to him. Passion is one thing that all high achievers have in common and to become a long-term performer you must embrace it if you want to reach greatness.

## What If I Don't Have a Passion?

When we don't spend much time focusing on our passions, they're often difficult to identify. But we all have passion; it's only a matter of discovering it. We have found six fundamental factors that determine when passion is present in yourself or any of your MVPs.

**1. Flow**: If you lose track of time while doing or thinking about something, you're in a state of passion.

**2. Failure**: You will persist despite failure when you're passionate

**3. Free**: We're not suggesting that you work for free, but the truth is that you go above and beyond when you're passionate about the outcome.

**4. Distraction**: Pay attention to what is distracting you, it could be a passion.

**5. Against the Grain**: A passion is something you're drawn to even when your MVPs are not. It's something you'd like to do even if it's not popular.

**6. Irritation**: Everyone has a short list of things that really annoy them when done poorly. Tune in; these are things you care about.

# Putting it to Work for You

How could you bring more of what you love into your life?

# SECTION II

# What
# They Want

# 7

## Everyone Sees Value Differently

Now that you have spent some time defining and clarifying what you value most, in the second section of the book we will turn our focus to understanding what your MVPs want.

You can increase your value to any MVP—your customer, boss, or loved one—if you are willing to watch and listen carefully, and ask informed questions about what they value most. Even for people you believe you know well, you may be surprised how remarkably different their view of the world may be from your own.

For example, how much do you know about whom your boss admires and values most in work and life? How much do you know about what your boss would consider his proudest moments? It's easy to assume, but instead of jumping to "logical" conclusions, find out for sure by doing your homework and talking with them about it. Do you have a clear sense of your best customers' biggest disappointments and setbacks? Their successes and failures—or good and bad experiences in any relationship—absolutely impact your MVPs' top priorities.

Everyone has a story about his or her career and life, and if you want to be valued, respected and admired by that MVP, then it's your job to be the detective who finds that out. What you will discover is not only their personal history in business and in life, but more important, what those experiences meant to them. The following advertising campaign brilliantly addresses this issue of perceptions:

***"The more you look at the world, the more you recognize that what one person values may be different from the next."***

This billboard appeared in international airports for many years as part of the thought-provoking "Different Values" ad campaign launched by one of the world's largest financial services firms. HSBC positioned itself

## EVERYONE SEES VALUE DIFFERENTLY

as the "worldwide local bank" – taking pride in understanding cultural differences and value systems. For any global company, this sensitivity means the difference between managing a prosperous, growing business and one that quickly becomes out of touch and is left behind by its customers. HSBC has revenues of over $100 billion and relationships with customers, employees, and managers in more than 80 nations where the company thrives. In today's global economy, anyone who does business around the world realizes that success or failure depends on how quickly and how intimately you can come to understand the different ways people see value. When you open your mind and heart to those differences, you can better meet those needs and be more sensitive to those viewpoints. Wouldn't that make you more trusted and valuable? In fact, why should someone value your opinion at all until you demonstrate that you understand theirs? It's a matter of reciprocity. You don't have to agree, but you will be more valuable if you understand these different viewpoints.

> Everyone has a life and a career story, and if you want to be valued, respected and admired, then it's your job to be the detective who finds that out.

By taking the time to discover the subtleties of how your MVPs define success, you will demonstrate interest and support for the things they value, and you will know what your MVPs are willing to support, defend, and fight for. If we don't know how our MVPs' values differ from our own, it's easy to see why we sometimes have conflicts as we pursue our goals. Knowledge is power, especially when it comes to giving and receiving value.

## ADMIRED

We have a dear friend whose decade-long marriage recently hit the rocks. This year is our 30th wedding anniversary, and he turned to us for advice, as nothing he'd thought of so far had worked. He claimed that he would "do anything" to get her back into his life. We asked him to name five things that his wife loves to do. He had absolutely no idea.

It's natural to feel frustrated that all our hard work has gone unrecognized and unrewarded, but often what we're doing isn't what the other person currently values (even if we think it *should* be). We asked our friend to think of five ways in which he could become more valuable to his wife as a lover, a friend, a partner, and a family member. How could he empower her to do what she loves? Those questions alone were an eye-opener for both of them, as they had never before invested time in thinking about the things they valued (or did not value!).

So understanding what your MVPs value, rather than relying on a default definition based on your own ideas and assumptions, gives you an advantage. It allows you to understand what they want in life, what motivates them, and how to reward them in a way that matches those values.

EVERYONE SEES VALUE DIFFERENTLY

# Putting It to Work for You

In chapter 3 we looked at the priorities of your MVPs. These will tell you a lot about what they value. We recommend that you schedule time to sit with key MVPs and ask them what they value. Here are some questions to guide that process.

What have been some high points in their life and what was valuable about those experiences?

.................................................................................................................

.................................................................................................................

.................................................................................................................

What have been some low points and what was upsetting about those experiences?

.................................................................................................................

.................................................................................................................

.................................................................................................................

Ask what you could do to be more valuable to them?

.................................................................................................................

.................................................................................................................

.................................................................................................................

## ADMIRED

Look at what they value. How could you bring more of what they love into their life?

..........................................................................................................................

..........................................................................................................................

..........................................................................................................................

In your address book, create a field for what they value. As you learn more about what your MVPs care about, make a note about it and think about how you can help them get more of that.

# 8

## The Power of Praise

What people want most from you is respect. But when it comes to giving feedback, we tend to avoid flattery and heap on "constructive" criticism in the name of improvement. Unfortunately, this is not the best way to motivate change in your MVPs or help them reach their goals. In fact, we have it all wrong, and by heaping on criticism and skimping on praise, not only do we *not* create value for others, we're also not getting any closer to being seen as more valuable to them.

## ADMIRED

Whether we're showing off a new outfit or a new breakthrough on a project, most of us enjoy the small and large thrills of everyday admiration. The bright bluish green "skin" I bought for my new Apple Air cost me $30. My technical friends giggled at the waste of money, and I would normally agree with them. However, my new accessory went from overpriced to more than worth the money the moment I pulled it out in a client meeting and people admired it. It looks cool, and I felt more chic than I did before. Yes, most of us are easily flattered for the decisions we make.

But does work-related flattery offer the same pick-me-up that a personal compliment does? Should we be "oh"ing and "ah"ing over our customers,' colleagues,' and employees' accomplishments? If you want them to be more engaged, successful, and efficient, *yes!* Studies show that praise does improve performance. (When you tell performers who work at an average level that they are "A" students, they tend to do better.)

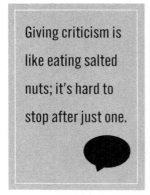

Giving criticism is like eating salted nuts; it's hard to stop after just one.

Unfortunately, praise is both harder for us to give and to receive than criticism. That is because humans are wired to watch for danger, and when we hear bad news our brain activates a fight or flight response, immediately assessing the situation to decide what to do next. As a result, if someone gives us a batch of lovely compliments and then one piece of criticism, it is that negative comment that our brains pick out and spends precious time and energy analyzing. On the flip side, because our ancient brain is trained to be critical of things that don't seem right, we tend to be way too critical of other people.

THE POWER OF PRAISE

## Avoid the Criticism Sandwich

Stanford professor Cliff Nass is an expert on responses to praise and criticism. His research reveals that delivering a *criticism sandwich*—specific praise before criticism and general praise afterward—is the wrong way to diffuse its impact. Because it takes so much brain power to analyze criticism, we don't remember anything said before it (this is called "retroactive interference"). But after hearing criticism our minds and bodies snap to attention, improving our memories (or "proactive enhancement"). So anything you say after criticizing someone is generally remembered.

Nass says giving criticism is like eating salted nuts; it's hard to stop after just one. The opposite is also true; we tend to deliver vague and scant positive remarks. Dr. Nass advises that you turn this on its head when evaluating your MVP. Give them one specific criticism in a way that they can take action to do something about it, and then a much longer list of praise. They'll feel better, remember the praise more easily, be more receptive to the criticism, and they'll feel more positively about you to boot.

The leaders we admire go out of their way to recognize, support, and reward the strengths of their people. It's in a leader's best interest to cheerlead a great performing team. Catch them in the act of doing things right. When you do that, the team will make more sacrifices on your behalf, come up with better ideas, and generally perform better. People admire leaders who *give* credit and *take* blame for the team.

## Flattery is Underrated

Cliff Nass' research indicates that flattery is highly underrated. When he asked two groups of students to play a guessing game with a computer,

# ADMIRED

he told half of them the computer would comment on the questions they asked and the other half, that the computer would spit out random comments unrelated to their questions. The computer praised both groups equally and sure enough, after the experiment, the group that had received random praise rated the interaction—and the computer itself—just as highly as did the other group.

Real flattery, rather than random, works even better. If you want to increase your value and be more admired, join the mutual admiration society. In his research on human and computer interaction, Nass found that computers that praised themselves were not as well received as computers that praised others. His participants also judged the computer that praised itself less competent than the computer that was praised by another. Nass concludes that the results are quite clear: "never praise yourself when you can have others do it for you."

In *The Man Who Lied to His Laptop*, Nass uses the example of praising the person who introduces him at a talk. He makes a point of beginning his speech by thanking the introducer and saying how much it means to be introduced by such a wonderful (fill in the blank). But it's important to make sure that the flattery isn't patronizing. Find something meaningful to you and the other person and make a very specific reference to their accomplishments or actions in that area. This leads to what Nass calls a "positive spiral." The research shows that your perceived mutual feelings of competence and confidence in each other will increase when you praise each other. Not only that but it leads the audience to perceive the introducer as more intelligent, and believe the praise heaped on you is even more valid.

Actively looking for and pointing out *legitimate* examples of excellence in others is leadership. And it makes you more valuable and admired.

THE POWER OF PRAISE

# Putting it to Work for You

At work, if you want your team to perform in a certain way, seek out those performing at the highest level and make their actions known to all by highlighting it in a specific way. Who could you praise today?

# 9

## Finding Common Ground

Ambassador Jan Eliasson—a longtime Swedish diplomat and UN Deputy Secretary General—laments the hundreds of thousands of lives that could have been saved had the UN's mediation missions been able to intervene in the long and bloody Iran-Iraq war. To prevent a resumption of the horrendous bloodshed, Eliasson used an unlikely approach to find what both sides believed were most valuable, just as you would with your dearest MVPs. He did his homework into the culture and history of the warring parties to see where there might be some hope for common ground.

# ADMIRED

The nations looked to sharia law to guide their decision about how to punish their former enemies, despite how weary they were about returning to battle. One side referenced a section of the Koran that said if a man broke into a neighbor's house he should be punished. They viewed the war as a kind of "breaking in" and thought the soldiers should each receive 20 lashes and the officers, 40 as spelled out in the Koran.

Wanting to avoid more bloodshed and help the factions begin to repair their communities, Eliasson's UN team returned to the negotiating table the following morning and read aloud another section of the Koran. This one said if a man turns his back to you, you should not attack him. The mood in the room changed almost instantly. Now instead of skeptical scowls, there were smiles around the table. The men took out their pocket Korans to check the source, nodding their approval.

More than twenty years later Eliasson can still remember one of the revolutionaries giving him a strong embrace and the feeling of the man's beard scratching his cheek. That simple act of mediating peace by thoughtfully considering all options based, not on their own culture, but on the Iranian's and Iraqi's, made all the difference. The mediators had acknowledged what mattered most, the deeper values and purpose of a people.

## Remember to Have Fun

According to our research, people who find meaning and engagement in their work report eight common traits they admire most in their leaders. Those characteristics include honesty, supportiveness, and cooperation, but also a sense of fun and a connection to family. When negotiations seem to be breaking down and everyone involved is feeling negative and out of energy, find a way to incorporate some of those eight principles.

FINDING COMMON GROUND

Eliasson recalls another trip when he was in Iran on a small matter of regional security—a matter he thought would be easily solved. Instead he spent three days there making almost no progress. Normally precise with his language, the frustrated Ambassador abruptly said he wanted to *break up* the meeting. He had meant to say he wanted "a break," but before he could rephrase them, his words were quickly translated into Farsi, and his counterparts thought he was ready to head to the airport.

> Even if you don't understand why it is important to them, doing something that is meaningful to your MVP will transform your relationship.

Puzzled and annoyed, the leader of the Iranian delegation asked him what he'd like to do instead, a good question Eliasson would have asked if the tables were turned. The Ambassador sighed, admitting that he had been to Tehran twenty times without a chance to sightsee and expressing a desire to visit an important cultural landmark: the carpet museum. They thought he might be patronizing them at first, until they realized he was serious.

Then one man said, "Well I'm from Tabriz and the museum has a special room for our carpets. If he insists on going, I'll be his guide." Another piped up, "I'm from Isfahan so I'll go with you and show him our carpets." They ended up spending three hours together exploring the museum, the Iranians explaining how the carpets were made, how the communities contribute to the task, and answering many other questions Eliasson had been wondering about.

When they returned to their negotiations at the ministry, the men had bonded. Suddenly positive and relaxed, they began referring to Eliasson

## ADMIRED

as "our friend." They hadn't thought that a westerner coming to Tehran would care that much about their culture.

Taking time to walk in the Iranian's shoes, and show his curiosity and respect for what was valuable to them on a personal level, forged deep and almost immediate bonds of trust for Eliasson and his new friends. He had the vision to understand how they wanted to be admired, and in turn, they admired him. Take the time to understand your MVPs' frame of mind, their personal history, background, and traditions. Even if you don't fully understand why it is important to them, doing something that is meaningful to your MVP will transform your relationship.

FINDING COMMON GROUND

## 💡 Charm is in the Eye of the Beholder

Whether you're mediating a peace agreement between warring nations or managing a team of colleagues, showing that you care about your MVP's values is a key component of building trust. But in a pinch, you can still have influence without knowing a thing about someone's traditions, family life, or favorite color.

In his book *The Man who Lied to his Laptop*, Cliff Nass describes an experiment he and a colleague conducted at Stanford University's Communication between Humans and Interactive Media (CHIMe) Lab. They were studying whether knowing a person's personality traits alone could guide you to a successful interaction with them. If you are an extrovert and want to influence a shy colleague, would matching his introverted traits make you more likeable? Social scientists call this theory "similarity-attraction;" it's the idea that "the more similar two people are, the more probable it is that they will like, trust, and respect each other." So when it comes to personality, do birds of a feather really flock together?

Nass discovered that they absolutely do. He invited participants to read and react to two differently worded eBay-style ads describing the same lamp for sale. The results showed that the more similar the buyer and seller, the more successful the sale. Extroverts who read the ad worded in an extroverted way, said they would pay more for that lamp than the one described in the "introverted" ad. And introverts preferred the ad with an introverted approach.

After conducting several other experiments in different contexts, Nass and his colleagues found proof, time and again, that there is no one winning personality type that can open all doors or charm all people. "Getting along with someone is not just a matter of being 'likable' or 'appropriate;' whether you share personality traits makes the difference." Matching communication styles was the secret to being friendly.

ADMIRED

# Putting it to Work for You

How could you show a genuine interest in the things your MVPs value?

.................................................................................................................

.................................................................................................................

.................................................................................................................

.................................................................................................................

.................................................................................................................

.................................................................................................................

.................................................................................................................

.................................................................................................................

.................................................................................................................

How could you give them more time to do what they love or support their passion?

.................................................................................................................

.................................................................................................................

.................................................................................................................

.................................................................................................................

.................................................................................................................

81

# SECTION III

# What
# They Want

# 10

## ACTION

In our journey to offer more value to the most important people in our lives and become admired and appreciated for what matters most, we have clarified our own goals and dug deeper into understanding our MVPs' desires and definitions of success. The next step is to get started doing something about it. We've isolated six main strategies to being admired: Action, Develop, Measure, Incentives, Recruit, and Excite.

Each strategy includes a number of tools that you can use to increase the value you give and receive. We'll begin with the tool #1 and the first rule of taking action: don't wait to be asked. Tool #2 is about how to find your

# ADMIRED

purpose and create more value for your MVPs. Tool #3 will explain why feeling guilty is a leadership trait and how you can put it to work for you. Tool #4 stresses the importance of gathering the right tools and creating a dedicated space to work on your goals.

ACTION / TOOL #1: DON'T WAIT TO BE ASKED

# Tool #1: Don't Wait to Be Asked

She gasped and struggled as the thug grabbed her from behind, locking her arms to her sides and lifting her feet off the ground, preventing the young girl from breaking free or hitting her assailant. In one horrible moment, all of the fighting tactics she had learned in martial arts classes were useless. She screamed miserably as she lost hope and he dragged her into the back of the car.

The self-defense instructor called the practice session to a halt and asked for suggestions. "Okay, class," she shouted. "She doesn't have her arms or her legs to fight, so tell me, what *does* she have?"

"Teeth" shouted one student. "Her head," another called out.

Challenges don't come neatly packaged the way we planned them. So when you're taken by surprise—and you don't have the tools or support that you'd counted on—the first thing to think about is not what you've lost, but what tools you still have. Start where you are. Figure out what you *do* have and use that to our advantage. When in doubt, take stock and then take action.

The most common reasons we freeze in a crisis—or simply procrastinate doing what we need to do to achieve our goals—is that we fear failure, don't know what to do, or we are emotionally overwhelmed by the tasks. The more innovative the goal or the greater the risks, the more reasons we find to stop us.

In *Waking the Tiger: Healing Trauma*, authors and therapists Peter Levine and Ann Frederick explain that people who are able to act during a crisis—even in the slightest way—are not as likely to experience post-traumatic stress syndrome. Action is what creates healing. By the same

## ADMIRED

token, if we are overwhelmed by the size or difficulty of any task, taking some action toward the solution will mellow the overwhelm. We will be better equipped to manage our emotions after even a few small actions.

## Lead, Even When Nobody's Watching

Action is great (and cheap) therapy, and according to actor and producer Sally Field, it's what saved her career and took her from the depths of depression and humiliation to Academy and Emmy awards. Her early success brought her work on television, but it also came with a lightweight girl-next-door image that was hard to shake. But Field didn't roll over and let her perky image limit her career. She worked on projects that mattered to her: first, the groundbreaking TV miniseries Sybil for, which she won an Emmy for her portrayal of a young woman suffering from multiple personalities after severe childhood abuse. (That's a far cry from the Flying Nun!) Three years later came the film Norma Rae with Field playing the title role of a single mother who helps unionize the cotton mill where she works. She won her first Academy Award for that film and proved her mettle once again.

The only thing you have power over is to get good at what you do.

Sally Field has been one of those rare women in Hollywood who has been a force for 40 years. But when we asked her how she decided to become a leader, Sally bristled. "That's a non-thing! Who wakes up one day and says, 'hmm, should I go to school or should I be a leader? I think I'm going to go out and lead,' she shook her head with sarcasm.

"The only thing you have power over is to get good at what you do. And the only way to become a leader is to have something to give back. And the only way to have something to give back is to get off your rear end and *do* something." You don't need a lofty goal, Field stresses. You simply need to be willing to "work your tail off and achieve something for yourself—some specific thing. But be excellent at it. That's the only way that you can be a leader."

In fact, she says, becoming a leader is rarely the original objective. It happens, sometimes "by accident, after you've pursued and struggled and kicked yourself around the block a zillion times. One day you look out and see what you've done in your life and suddenly people begin turning to you and saying, 'Lead us.' Huh?" For Field, becoming a leader in her industry came just like that, as a surprise after years of dedication to her passions and goals.

## You Won't Regret Taking Initiative

In our 2012 national survey, the participants who were most engaged in their work said they wanted their leaders to be ambitious and hardworking. After 500 conversations, the highly accomplished people we've spoken to certainly fit that description. In fact, from all of them we heard only one real regret about their careers: if anything, they wished they had moved faster or sooner to take action.

Sally Field didn't wake up one morning and decide to be a leader, nor did she wait to be invited or ask permission to play at a higher level in her profession. She took action not by dwelling on what everyone thought of her or what box they tried to keep her in, but moving toward her goal of becoming an accomplished actress and a serious industry professional—someone to be admired for something that matters to her. And she has.

## ADMIRED

### 💡 You don't have to be perfect to do something great

On our tour, meeting some of the worlds most admired and valued people, it was healing to learn that they are far from perfect, and none are admired or valued by everyone. I (Bonita) wish I knew when I started out that you don't have to be perfect to do something great. Countless times I've gotten in my own way thinking that perfection was required before launching an idea. And I spent too much of my youth feeling inadequate, routinely pulling the plug on my efforts before taking them public. In school, my papers would come back bloodied with red ink because I have dyslexia. And that would reinforce just how imperfect I was. So I took it as a message that I had nothing to contribute or say.

When you meet and study the world's highest achievers, you realize that most started out in life and work, flawed in their thinking, lacking skills, and often humiliated by inadequacies. Worse yet, there is always a choir of critics delighted to trumpet their failures along the way. No one is perfect, and no one who has ever done anything worthwhile, ever has been. High achievers focus on having impact and making a difference no matter how incomplete they are. The only thing you have control over is getting better every time you play.

ACTION / TOOL #1: DON'T WAIT TO BE ASKED

# Putting it to Work for You

Count your assets. What could you do this moment, with the skills and tools that you have, to move you forward toward your goal?

........................................................................................................

........................................................................................................

What actions can you take right now to build and enhance your network, skills, or talents? Calendar those actions!

........................................................................................................

........................................................................................................

Think about a task or goal that you can never seem to cross off your to do list. How important is it in reaching your goal? Could you change the goal to incorporate more fun? (If it's fun you are much more likely to do it.)

........................................................................................................

........................................................................................................

........................................................................................................

........................................................................................................

........................................................................................................

ADMIRED

# Tool #2: Create Value

"I wasn't too frightened about leaving college," Bill Gates reflected on his first year in business when I interviewed him at the World Economic Forum in Davos. "What bothered me was when all these people I'd recruited to leave their secure jobs to come work for my little startup were now actually expecting to get paid!"

Anyone who has created value—and eventually earned some respect and admiration for what they do—has had the realization that Gates did. The dream is free, but the journey is expensive. Whether you're a homemaker starting a micro-business or an executive taking that next promotion, the weight of having to create value in a new way can prevent any of us from welcoming a positive new challenge.

Intimidated by the task, we often let ourselves believe we're not as talented, connected, or wealthy as the achievers and entrepreneurs who went before us. Of course, for most people embarking on a new challenge, none of this is true. (Even Steve Jobs began with no endowment.) The majority of people who want to create value don't receive the opportunity wrapped up in a bow, and when they eventually earn the recognition they deserve, it is only after great turmoil.

## Value Trumps Talent Every Time

There are great singers waiting tables and brilliant engineers toiling away in mechanic shops. Becoming a success is not about having enough talent; it's about taking action to create value for others. It's not even about being right or wrong, good or bad. Plenty of great products have failed, losing out to others with inferior design, technology, or service.

## ACTION / TOOL #2: CREATE VALUE

And plenty of other managers who have half your talent are valued more by their company than you are by yours. The difference between those who "make it big" and those who don't is the ability to create value for your customer and your boss.

As investors, we have bet our life savings on courageous entrepreneurs who have a passion for learning what their customers value. We've funded and coached profitable startups, and helped open nonprofit entrepreneurship centers in challenging parts of the world. We've poured our time and money into more than a dozen different types of enterprises, from a semiconductor to social media companies, from firms fighting cancer to rental real estate, movie theatres, and even Broadway shows. None of these entrepreneurs 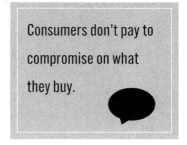 were born with a silver spoon, and neither were we. Some of these folks had fancy degrees, but none of the businesses came with a guarantee. In every case we have been deeply moved by how people without substantial money or extraordinary prior experience in a field can still add enormous value and have a huge impact on the world.

That is certainly true for a 3-year-old startup bootstrapped by two sisters called A Lot To Say. It's an apparel firm that turns recycled bottles and other garbage into eco-friendly fashion that's made in America. At first we thought the idea sounded really cool, but naïve as a viable business. We thought it was doomed until seeing and feeling the rich, luxuriously soft fabrics. They employ new technology that doesn't use toxic substances or waste endless gallons of water. As a result the clothes feel silky and look like a million bucks. In fact, you may have seen their stuff featured at the Grammy's, Sundance Film Festival, or in the Fred Segal's chic retail flagship store in Santa Monica.

**ADMIRED**

Founders Jennifer Stanich Banmiller and Allison Stanich Power didn't know the clothing business, although they did love fashion. One had been an executive in the pharmaceutical industry and the other had a marketing firm. They had never manufactured or distributed garments, although they had a strong moral drive to find non-toxic, non-polluting ways to make beautiful clothing.

## The Power of Starting from Scratch

"We didn't know how to do this thing," the A Lot to Say founders acknowledged. As risky as that sounds, the sisters had the humility to learn from experts. "We kept our heads and heart open every step of the way," they insisted, recruiting people with knowledge about everything from eco-manufacturing technology to retail merchandising.

We (Bonita and Mark) have discovered in our role as venture investors and executive coaches that the greatest breakthroughs in creating value often come from a beginner's mind. Whether you're working for a Fortune 500 firm or starting a new company, it's often powerful to start from scratch, free of prior psychological baggage and experiences.

On the other hand, that's a lot harder than paving the cow path! A Lot to Say didn't show up on the founders' doorstep as a nice neat business opportunity. The sisters didn't have the benefit of buying a franchise with a roadmap, suppliers, and a marketing plan. Like most startups, they had to begin creating value with the first product and the first customer and make progress one step at a time. That can be tedious and disheartening unless you're buoyed by a passion for the work and the purpose it represents.

## ACTION / TOOL #2: CREATE VALUE

## Customers Don't Pay to Compromise—Even for a Good Cause

For a venture with a social mission like A Lot to Say, it would have been tempting for Banmiller and Power to focus more on ecology than the customer experience. But the brutal truth is that the customer won't care for long about your intentions unless the product also looks and feels great. Consumers don't pay to compromise on what they buy.

And while it's expensive to invest in quality in the process of creating value, it's more risky not to do this. The garments must be chic and fashionable, not just non-toxic or made in America. "The customer doesn't care about all the many complex things you have to do to get everything right. And even if it's a good cause, it still ultimately needs to feel sexy, accessible, and luxurious to customers," they sighed.

Whole Foods Markets would have not revolutionized the organic foods business if their mission was only to do good for the environment and be fair to labor. The food had to taste better, too. In *Success Built to Last*, we call this the *Genius of the And* versus the *Tyranny of the Or*. Whole Foods had to exceed the standards of quality by both the old measures that customers knew and loved *and* by the new measures that they aspired to create.

## Screw Business As Usual

We learned about A Lot to Say when I (Mark) was reviewing entries as one of six global judges selected by Richard Branson for his Virgin Unite entrepreneurship competition. What made Sir Richard's event different is that all the startups that entered were equally committed to a social mission as they were to creating a profitable business, a concept that's been catching momentum in recent years and becoming bankable.

## ADMIRED

When we do something meaningful to you that also does good for others, you work twice as hard at it. But if your heart isn't in what you do everyday, you'll burn out much faster, become less creative, and make more mistakes. It's hard to create value if you don't care—and it's almost impossible for others to value you when you feel that way.

This new attitude is what our cheeky friend Branson—whose heart is as big as his genius for building brands—irreverently calls *Screw Business as Usual*. He and his Virgin Unite Foundation are driving a social movement of entrepreneurs and corporate managers who believe it's in their enlightened self-interest to create value in their career, and in doing so create more value in a businesses that does well (financially) and does good (for the world). The breakthrough idea here is that it's not one or the other. It's both.

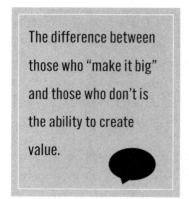

The difference between those who "make it big" and those who don't is the ability to create value.

When our national survey revealed that Americans feel a disconnect between what's meaningful in their life and their career ambitions, it made sense that most respondents said they are disengaged in their work. But there's a cure. You will be more courageous in following your dreams, and feel hugely engaged in your work and creating value if you're doing work that matters to you.

"I've felt overwhelmed on too many occasions to count," Branson sighed as he shared photos of his cherished home burning down. It was not the first time he had his a dream blown away. More than 350 companies carry the Virgin Brand, but many more than that many have failed to survive. If it had been easy for Branson, he would not be nearly so inspiring as a leader. Even when they're bored, scared, disappointed, or

## ACTION / TOOL #2: CREATE VALUE

exhausted, successful leaders cling to the knowledge that their time is limited and focus intensely on contributing value and remaining creative.

## How to Build Value

The secret to creating value is to find some mission that speaks to you. When you do, you'll have more energy and courage to do something that other people value, respect and eventually, admire. It doesn't have to be world hunger; but it does have to be personal to you and useful to other people who will hire you or buy the product. Welcome advice. Take one step at a time.

Here are nine strategies for isolating what is meaningful to you and building more value into your work:

**Value Builder #1: Don't try to be all things to all people.**

Trying to serve too many MVPs only results in you adding less value to more people. Be clear about who you want to be valuable to. Help those people define their success and achieve it.

**Value Builder #2: Be simple, convenient, and usable**

Focus on making the service or product as easy to use and intuitive as possible. Think about what you want your target audience to be, do, or have. How could you help them achieve that? Observe how your target audience uses what you have to sell and how they solve problems.

**ADMIRED**

## Value Builder #3: Get Known & Showcase what is valuable

How are you getting the word out about what you do? How are you presenting yourself or your services in a way that makes it attractive to customers?

## Value Builder #4: Give a sense of security

Protect what is your target audience believes is valuable.

## Value Builder #5: Make it personal

Build trust –honesty, responsiveness and reliability /consistency

Give it a face

Give it a personality

## Value Builder #6: Build Community

encourage open communication

encourage participation

Encourage ownership

## Value builder #7: Define "quality"

Your customer may define "quality" differently than you do. For some retail items, for example, quality may mean that something looks chic or

## ACTION / TOOL #2: CREATE VALUE

expensive, not whether it's the most advanced technology.

**Value builder #8: Be in the right place at the right time**

To be available to your customer you've got to be where they are. It's also good career advice: We have a dear friend who wanted to be a Hollywood writer and producer. It was much easier for him to pursue that dream once he moved to Southern California so that he could actually meet with and learn from the people involved in that industry.

**Value builder #9: Dump the mission statement**

Instead create a manifesto that is real to your customer and that you and your team actually believe and are willing to be held responsible to deliver. Here's A Lot To Say's manifesto:

*If you think something, say it.*

*If you believe something, say it.*

*If you want something, say it.*

*Because saying it creates new awareness.*

*Awareness sparks new behavior.*

*And new behavior inspires us all to be better.*

*if we speak out, others will act out.*

*To vote. Recycle. Save.*

*To think a little more.*

*To try a little harder.*

*To live more honestly.*

## ADMIRED

*Thoughtfully. Joyfully.*

*You have a lot to say.*

*So never be afraid to say it.*

*Or wear it.*

*Everyday.*

ACTION / TOOL #2: CREATE VALUE

### Customized Value: The New Competitive Edge

Two centuries ago bookmaking was a time-consuming art whose finished product was expensive and accessible only to an elite few. Today, *anyone* can take charge of the printing press. You can publish online, create an eBook and zap it to the world, or even print your own physical book. In fact, bestselling authors like Seth Godin say they will never use a traditional publisher again.

And not just individuals, but companies and teams now have more power than ever to deliver value to their customers in a personal way. At TED we met a scientist who uses patients' cells to "print out" new organs for them, creating a perfect fit that their immune system won't reject.

At Stanford engineering lab, students print out 3D prototypes for new products just a few moments after they imagine them. When you can print out plastic, metal, and wooden products on local laser printers—and test many different options to see what really works for customers—you will save months and millions over making one expensive prototype, manufacturing millions and then hoping it will sell.

As our means of production become more automated, customized and local, the competitive edge for the 21st century will no longer lie in how big your company is but in how well you can accurately assess what customers value and build exactly that. The time and cost associated with tooling products is plummeting. This means you can get exactly what you want, when you want it, with less cost, raw materials and shipping. Businesses that can quickly determine what customers value and fill that need will be the winners on this new playing field.

# Tool #3: Guilt Is Good

Just as the jet was lifting off, the bang of a sudden explosion and black smoke billowing out of the wing sent the passengers into hysterics. The plane was filled with employees, customers, and press to celebrate the first flight of a new airline, but instead they were now the screaming witnesses of an engine bursting into flames. The aircraft banked to make an emergency landing using the remaining three engines on the 747. It was the inaugural flight of Virgin Atlantic.

Reflecting on the day years later, Virgin owner Sir Richard Branson quipped: "No one likes to hear a big bang when you're taking off, particularly when it's an inspection!" Virgin had never been in the aviation business before, and the company had confidently trumpeted the launch with brilliant irony on London and New York billboards: *Virgin: We have more experience than our name would suggest.* In classic Virgin business strategy, Branson started the airline to take advantage of what he saw as a big gap in service left by an entrenched competitor. He was bent on giving customers a better experience. "This wasn't what I had in mind!" Branson teased.

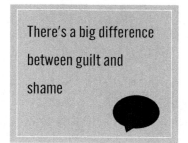

There's a big difference between guilt and shame

The engine wasn't insured, and so Branson was "a million dollars down" on day one of his new venture. He came home from the event to find his bank manager sitting on his doorstep with the intention to put "the Virgin group out of business." Branson threw the banker out of his house and got a new one who supported his intention to get the airline up and running. It was a matter of pride and guilt. "I couldn't face letting down

## ACTION / TOOL #3: GUILT IS GOOD

all those employees or customers."

## The Guilty Get Things Done

Surprisingly, a new study has found that proneness to feel guilt like Branson did is a very admirable trait and, in fact, predicts your likelihood to be chosen as a leader people want to follow and admired for your attitude. First of all, no one expects or believes you can be perfect—and thank goodness for that! But there's a big difference between *guilt* and *shame*, according to Stanford researchers. When you admit guilt, you're publically demonstrating a desire to be responsive and make things right,

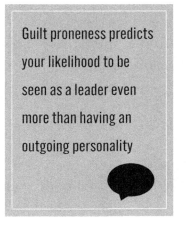

Guilt proneness predicts your likelihood to be seen as a leader even more than having an outgoing personality

which is an admired trait. Instead, if you languish in shame, you'll tend to focus more on yourself and how bad you feel without addressing the needs of others or the issue at hand.

Stanford researchers pinpointed "guilt versus shame proneness" in individuals by asking a group of complete strangers to fill out an online personality quiz. The participants rated how they would react to specific blunders, like spilling wine on the cream-colored carpet at a co-worker's housewarming. Then the researchers asked these same strangers to come to a classroom and spend one hour together performing two group tasks. The scientists didn't assign a leader. When the group completed the tasks, the participants rated one another on leadership qualities—taking charge, for example, and leading the conversation.

ADMIRED

In all the groups tested, the people who were most likely to be deemed leaders were the same ones who had scored highest in guilt proneness. Guilt proneness predicted an individual's likelihood to be seen as a leader even more than having an outgoing personality, which has long been assumed a popular leadership trait. Being an extrovert or having a bubbly personality may be useful in many aspects of life, but others admire you more for your willingness to be accountable and for being gracious about and responsive to your mistakes.

When the participants in the Stanford studies evaluated each other's performance, they clearly preferred the guilt-prone folks as leaders because they appeared to work harder to give all the members an opportunity to speak and be understood, and at the same time they seemed to lead the task and take responsibility for the outcomes. "Guilt-prone people tend to carry a strong sense of responsibility to others, and that responsibility makes other people see them as leaders," says Becky Schaumberg, a doctoral candidate in organizational behavior who conducted the research with Francis Flynn, the Paul E. Holden Professor of Organizational Behavior at the Stanford Graduate School of Business.

Guilt may feel bad to you, but your pain is perceived by others as willingness to do something about it. When guilt causes you to do what's good for others, particularly at personal cost, you're seen as a leader.

## Strange Bedfellows: Guilt and Long-term Success

We saw the same results when we interviewed famous leaders, from the presidents of nations to Nobel laureates. For our book *Success Built to Last*, we conducted a "World Success Survey" with Wharton Business School, and Mark also lead hundreds of face-to-face meetings with leaders who had been noteworthy in their fields or professions a minimum of 20 years. These long-term high achievers—from the Dalai

## ACTION / TOOL #3: GUILT IS GOOD

Lama to Steve Jobs—represented over 100 nations.

We asked what three things they wished they'd known at the beginning of their careers. Surprisingly, these mega-successful leaders all lamented how hard it was to narrow it down to only three missteps or lessons learned from mistakes. They talked about failure so much you'd think they were losers! Bestselling author Dr. John Maxwell sighed: "It would be easier to give you two or three hundred things I would have done better than just two or three!"

Whether they are running a single household, saving a community, or managing a multinational corporation, the individual responses were consistent. When you make a mistake, your credibility soars if you show guilt and take action to fix it. You'll not only feel better, but you'll endear yourself to others with your humanity when you have the courage to try your best to make things right.

But when it comes to fixing a mistake, remember the three R's.

**1. Responsibility:** People admire you more when you raise your hand to be accountable. While guilt isn't considered a positive emotion, when it's followed by constructive action, it's a home run for your credibility.

When something goes wrong and you're in a position to take responsibility, do it immediately. Then quickly get to work discovering what the MVP in the situation is most concerned about, and how to remedy the situation in the way that best addresses them. This is another golden opportunity to show your MVP that you can be trusted and valued even when you make a mistake.

**2. Responsiveness:** Even if you don't know the answer to a question being asked of you, respond with your total commitment to making things right. (Your lawyer may not agree with this, but it will win you long-term respect and admiration.) Silence is *not* golden in this case. No

# ADMIRED

one interprets a long silence as an indication that good news may be coming.

Imagine you asked a loved one, "Do you love me?" and they hesitated in even the slightest way. How would you feel? Our primal brain center, the amygdala, is hardwired to the fight-or-flight response and desperate for an instant response to emotionally charged questions like that. The longer you wait to do something about your mistake, the more others will feel you've violated their trust. When a loved one asks you a question try your best to focus on only them to avoid hesitation. Observe your interactions with your loved ones for one week. What did you notice about your responsiveness?

**3. Reliability:** Be consistent with your promises. People like to feel they can rely on who you are (even if you're odd), so consistency is cherished more than charisma.

While most of us would prefer to be judged by our good intentions, that's not usually how others evaluate us. Intentions are important, but outcomes are much easier to judge. More often than not, people will believe your intentions only after you've actually done something about your mistake. This is the moment of truth when others will decide who you are and whether or not they can count on you. So when you make a promise to your MVP, make it your top priority and take the steps necessary to deliver.

ACTION / TOOL #4: THE RIGHT TOOL FOR THE JOB

# Tool #4: The Right Tool for the Job

When I (Bonita) was seven, my parents mysteriously removed all the furniture from the cramped living room in our tiny apartment. It was 1965 and America was in a hot-headed race for space. Dad sawed and hammered a structure out of spare lumber that at first looked like a launch pad, and in many ways would end up serving that purpose for the three of us kids. It was the place from which we launched our dreams.

The project soon consumed the room, and on every surface my folks painted pictures of spacecraft, math formulas, chemical equations and parts of speech. It's no surprise I never had the urge to write on the walls as a kid; there wasn't room left after my parents had done that for me. What emerged from the sweat and sawdust was a massive cabinet with three workspaces for my two older brothers and me to study. Each section of the desk had pegboard hooks to hang scissors and stylus, along with shelves to organize books and study supplies. Everyday when I came home from school there was no doubt what I would do that night. The first thing I saw even before the kitchen, bathroom or bedroom was the place where I would conquer my homework.

My parents never lectured me about school. They had created an environment that was obsessed with its importance. My desk was a rocket ship with a dashboard and seat to pilot my dreams. My folks didn't have to post a mission statement. They guided us kids to the *learning altar* in the middle of the house, and we spent endless hours every day playing with everything we could learn. They gave me the tools that, in my father's eyes, would assure I would never go without a meal, as he often had.

ADMIRED

## Learning the Skills for Success

My father grew up in not much more than a wood shack outside Detroit without floors, indoor plumbing, or heating. With nine kids in the house there wasn't enough food to go around so those who loitered went without. The habit stuck. So when he had a family of his own and we sat down to dinner as a family, my father inhaled his supper and then began asking each of us to recount the best thing we learned in school that day. He took in every piece of knowledge we gained just as eagerly as he had his food. Rich discussions ensued.

Dad was 17 before he enjoyed three square meals in a day—or even slept in a real bed—and those conveniences came only because he'd enlisted in the Navy. Unlike his fellow recruits who complained about the austere and demanding military environment, Fritz felt the Service provided luxury he'd never before imagined. At the top of the list of perks was a chance at a formal education. Navy schools were famously practical at giving people skills you could take to the bank, enabling Dad to find his talent for fixing and building things, from cars and houses to Naval aircraft. He realized that education was his ticket out of poverty, and that discovery transformed his life and mine forever.

> When you set your sights on a goal that really matters to you, create a dedicated workspace for that project.

My dad says his construction project in the living room had started out simply to be a desk, but it clearly exploded with his greater ambitions. There was no greater gift Dad could imagine giving his family than a place like that, where we could express our potential.

Though both of us paid our way through school and struggled with

## ACTION / TOOL #4: THE RIGHT TOOL FOR THE JOB

dyslexia, our future had been nearly preordained. Our folks had erased any doubt that we'd finish school. They created in us a mindset that education was our ticket to financial and creative freedom, and that goal became irresistible. It was this kind of you-can-make-your-dreams-come-true-WHEN-you-get-the-skills attitude that built America in the first place. It's what drives the extraordinary success of every culture that embraces this belief in all of the roaring global emerging markets—from China, India, and Brazil, to Israel, Jordan, and Korea. Mom and Dad put this core mission front and center in our lives. There was nothing more important to us. Even with lack of money and learning disabilities working against us, our families' obsession with education transformed the odds. What should have been unlikely success for us became unavoidable.

## Make the Space for Your Goals

When you set your sights on a goal that really matters to you—something for which you wish to be respected, valued and admired—create a dedicated workspace for that project. There you can indulge your urge to take action, day or night. Whenever inspiration strikes, you will literally have the space to get it done. This doesn't mean you need to set up a room for every goal; it does mean you will be more successful if you create a reliable location to put all the tools you need to do the job. That could be a binder, a computer file, a bookshelf, closet, side table, or even a big plastic bin.

It doesn't need to be an apartment-sized desk like the one my dad built, but we encourage you to create a shrine, a tangible place to put all the resources necessary to help you practice and get good at what you do. Everyone needs a workbench—metaphorically or physically—where you can invest in your passion and spend time and energy crafting your dream.

ADMIRED

# Putting It to Work for You

What changes to your work environment would support your team in taking meaningful action toward the goal?

......................................................................................................................

......................................................................................................................

......................................................................................................................

What tasks need to be done to achieve the goal?

......................................................................................................................

......................................................................................................................

......................................................................................................................

Where will you complete those tasks?

......................................................................................................................

......................................................................................................................

......................................................................................................................

What resources are available to perform the necessary tasks – particularly those tasks that need to be done daily or weekly?

......................................................................................................................

......................................................................................................................

......................................................................................................................

How could you make those tools so conveniently laid out that there is no

## ACTION / TOOL #4: THE RIGHT TOOL FOR THE JOB

impediment to getting the work done? For example, if you want to read more books on your profession, could you use your drive time to listen to books, listen while you exercise or set up a great reading chair by a shelf with those books?

........................................................................................................................

........................................................................................................................

........................................................................................................................

What could you do to decorate your office so it gives you energy to work , passion and action toward the tasks necessary to deliver for MVPs?

........................................................................................................................

........................................................................................................................

........................................................................................................................

What changes could you make in your work environment to communicate to your clients what you're there to do for them?

........................................................................................................................

........................................................................................................................

........................................................................................................................

# 11

## DEVELOP

Taking action is an essential and motivating first step toward realizing your goals and adding value to the most important people in your life. Now that you have some momentum, begin investing time and resources in developing your skills and passions. Tool #5 stresses the importance of focusing on the moment and giving 100 percent in your current role, even if it's not your dream job. Tool #6 will inspire you to invest in yourself and your passions. Tool #7 shows why focusing on righting a wrong may not be the most effective way to achieve your goals. Tool #8 is about sticking to your goals even if the critics don't share your vision.

# Tool #5: Start Where You Are

When we're focused on our ambitions, it's easy to be seduced by delusions of grandeur and forget to be excellent at what we're doing right this moment. The brutal truth is people won't remember if you liked this job or whether you were on your way to greater things. They'll only remember how well (or poorly) you worked with them. If you want to be admired and respected, demonstrate your value in the job you do today.

In our interviews with the world's highest achievers one after another told us how important it is to do your job better than anyone has before you. "Do it like you're going to have it forever," Jeff Immelt advised over coffee one afternoon. Don't spend all your energy and talent focused on "the next job; learn something—learn a lot—about the job you have today. First go deep, then go broad." First develop a skill set and demonstrate that you're good at it, and then you'll earn the attention to be offered more opportunities. For the first seven or eight years of his career, Immelt worked in sales as a sales, marketing, and product manager. Before he hoped to become an executive he "built a trade and had the skills to show for it. I can make a sales call as well as anyone in the company."

Immelt encourages people to do every job well. Build a reputation as a trustworthy person and a hard worker. "Do it well and with integrity. Instead of thinking that or behaving like a job is beneath you, add value every step along the way."

## DEVELOP / TOOL #5: START WHERE YOU ARE

## Create a Solid Foundation for Success

Tom Moran had that work ethic from the time he was a teenager in his first job as a janitor at his own high school. He was going to be the best he could be at that. He then became a master French fry man at Nathan's, then a short order cook at a dental factory, a pizza delivery boy, a cemetery worker, and a taxi cab driver. Along the way he poured himself into the job at hand and got a reputation for being great at whatever he was doing.

And what, exactly, is he doing these days? Tom Moran is the president and CEO of Mutual of America, one of the few investment and insurance giants that was unshaken during the financial crisis. His journey to the top may have started a long way down, but he says, "All of that was exactly what I needed to get to the position I'm in now."

> People are so busy looking for the perfect job or dream opportunity they forget to pay attention to the job they have.

Ironically, people are so busy looking for the perfect job or dream opportunity they forget to pay attention to the job they have. The MVPs in your life—your customers, colleagues, and your boss—will remember if you tried your best and treated others with respect. They'll want to help you as you helped them and that may mean an amazing job opportunity or key connection that changes your life forever. On the other hand no one will thank you for keeping one foot out the door, waiting for your chance to move on to a better place. And opportunities might just pass you by because of it. If you don't feel you can add value where you are, think about where you could add value and get yourself there.

ADMIRED

# Putting it to Work for You

What are the elements of your job where you can build skills for your dream job? How could you develop those skills?

........................................................................................................................

........................................................................................................................

........................................................................................................................

........................................................................................................................

........................................................................................................................

# Tool #6: Invest in Yourself

Life's pleasant inertia kept Brad Buell a successful grocery guy for a dozen years. Brad was the friendly, patient clerk with handsome blue eyes who could help you find anything in his well-stocked milk box. In his head he kept a virtual catalog of where every product belonged. Brad was an expert at what he did, having spent almost two decades perfecting momentary interactions with customers, day after day, checking items, stocking the ultimate dairy selection and helping people get what they needed in quick, efficient, satisfying transactions.

But Brad hit the wall one Christmas when his boss wouldn't let him commit to a long needed vacation, something for which he had saved for a year. His frustration finally inspired him to consider moving on from his otherwise comfortable job. Brad wasn't sure what to do next, but took a leap of faith—not to change everything all at once, but to enjoy one of his passions in a deeper way. He was a voracious reader, and had grown up with an aptitude for algebra, puzzles, and historical facts. He remembered how much he had enjoyed computer programming towards the end of his degree at San Jose State University, and his frustrations at work were just the nudge he needed to re-enroll in the community college.

At first he was overwhelmed at being back in a classroom. Some of the homework assignments were daunting, technology had changed a zillion times since he had finished school in the 70s, and he was still working full time. But Brad stuck with it, and after two years of night classes, he graduated with an associates degree in computer science. With a wealth of experience on the frontline as a grocer, he was an ideal new member of the supermarket's IT group, where he spent the next nine years—no longer freezing in the milk box.

## Trusting Your Instincts Pays Off

It's rare to find a systems architect who is as warm and personable as Brad is technically competent. It was no surprise he was recruited by a company named Fortune Magazine's most admired firm in its industry. Today management have added Brad to a list of the most valued IT professionals in their global $2.2 billion company. He's admired for something that matters to him.

> For many of us, it takes a disappointment or some other shake up to get us out of our comfort zone and wake up to the greater possibilities that await us.

With the new confidence that came from bringing his passions to life in his daily work, Brad found his soul mate at age 39, and they now have a son and a daughter together. He moved from the trailer park he had called home for four years to a brand new custom-built, two-story home smack in the middle of California's pricey Silicon Valley.

For many of us, it takes a disappointment or some other shake up to get out of our comfort zone (or rut) and wake up to the greater possibilities that await us. Our biggest contribution to the world can lay dormant for years until it is awakened by outside forces. After all, you have to make a living, and once you find a good enough job that pays the bills, it's terribly hard to risk your livelihood. Without the proverbial burning platform, it's difficult to make such a major change even if you think you could trade up to a more valuable venture that fills you with passion.

## DEVELOP / TOOL #6: INVEST IN YOURSELF

Investing in yourself means you spend your time, money, attention, and talent on what you want to build. It means getting skills, building community, and obtaining the resources necessary to make your goal happen.

We've learned first hand that investing in yourself and your passion is not a distraction or a waste of time. It's the only way to become great at what you do. In our global studies with world leaders, we've seen over and over that the only way to do your best work is to employ as many of your passions as possible to get it done. By trusting his instinct about what he loved—and becoming more skilled at that passion—Brad created a win-win for his career, his company, and his life.

ADMIRED

# Putting it to Work for You

What 1 skill could you acquire that would make you more valuable in each of your major roles?

......................................................................................................................

......................................................................................................................

......................................................................................................................

What could you do to build each skill that would benefit you?

......................................................................................................................

......................................................................................................................

......................................................................................................................

What community or professional association would help support your developing skills?

......................................................................................................................

What books, magazines, or websites could keep you up-to-date?

......................................................................................................................

......................................................................................................................

What friends could help you in that field or profession?

......................................................................................................................

......................................................................................................................

### DEVELOP / TOOL #6: INVEST IN YOURSELF

What resources (money, space, time) will you need to invest in yourself?

.................................................................................................................

.................................................................................................................

.................................................................................................................

.................................................................................................................

Calendar the action steps you will take to invest in yourself.

ADMIRED

# Tool #7: Live What You Are For

Spirit of America founder Jim Hake noticed that when American troops ignored Afghan communities that were destroyed in battle, more U.S. soldiers were ambushed and killed in those neighborhoods than in communities where American forces provided valuable aid. Better relations reduced conflict and saved lives. With that inspiration, Hake reinvented how, our troops interact with the local populations.

Doing this gave the army something to stand *for* rather than against. Their mission was no longer just to seek out and kill terrorists, it was to secure the community so we would not help create more terrorists. When the Army shows that their role is to build a safe community, the community is more eager to keep our soldiers safe and help them be more effective at achieving long-term security and peace.

## You Get What You Focus On

During a war, of course the strategy is to attack until you prevail. But you have to remember all along what you're hoping to achieve after the monster is gone, and not become a monster yourself. In any endeavor, it's easy to focus more on what you're against rather than what you hope to achieve—to become fixated on what's wrong or unfair. It's human nature to shoot first and ask questions later or feel tempted to crush anything that gets in the way of what we know is correct But living like a warrior under attack can also become a self-fulfilling prophecy. The best way to create any habit is practice, and it can be counter-productive to our goals and well-being if we spend all of our energy living for what we're against, rather than living for how you want your world and your life to be. You get what you focus on. A perpetually negative attitude can make us terrorists of a sort, repelling those around us and creating new enemies soon after the last one was destroyed.

We get stuck living for what we are against because that idea can seem so much grander than the reality of what we can achieve in one lifetime, at least initially. For example, if I'm against world hunger—Wow, that's big. But if I focus on what I'm for, well, then I can only afford to feed three children. Though your outcome may be smaller and require more effort, when you work toward what you are for, you will be more effective at achieving something meaningful.

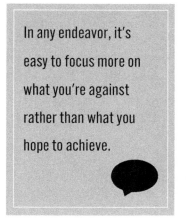

> In any endeavor, it's easy to focus more on what you're against rather than what you hope to achieve.

## Creation Is a Powerful Force

In Peter Ackerman and Jack DuVall's book *A Force More Powerful*, two political scientists analyze 20th century revolutions. They wondered about the differences between revolutions that produced democratic governments and those that yielded totalitarian ones. The main difference between the two was that the revolutions that focused on what the new government would look like—down to what departments and processes they would put in place—were more likely to result in more democratic governments and stronger economies.

Revolutions that erupt without much thought toward the design of the new government, may succeed at over-throwing injustice but they will be faced with a governmental void. That void is frequently filled by those thirsty for power. So revolutions that violently spring up tend to end with even bigger bullies taking over.

## ADMIRED

When someone sees an injustice and uses their anger to plot out the details of the solution—rather than the destruction of the bad guy in power—they're more effective at creating a new and positive place. The focus is on the solution rather than only the injustice. Whether your revolution is about the design of a new government or a better diet program, thinking through what you want to create is always more powerful than focusing solely on the injustice.

**DEVELOP / TOOL #7: LIVE WHAT YOU ARE FOR**

# Putting It To Work for You

Creating a life that matters means we must fight a few necessary battles, but not get trapped in Groundhog's Day, perpetuating our own circle of negativity. Creating a life that matters is the culmination of living, practicing, and focusing on what we want to build that is meaningful to us everyday.

Think about your most important goals. Do they reflect what you want to create or what you want to destroy?

...........................................................................................................................

...........................................................................................................................

...........................................................................................................................

What bugs you most?

...........................................................................................................................

...........................................................................................................................

What does your rant tell you about what you value?

...........................................................................................................................

...........................................................................................................................

How could you take action to set goals that are for that value?

...........................................................................................................................

...........................................................................................................................

...........................................................................................................................

## ADMIRED

What are the details of your solution? What standards do you want to live up to? Who are the people you will need to help you? What are the issues you will need the skills to address?

## Tool #8: Be Misunderstood

Successful people who are admired long-term for something that matters are willing to be misunderstood in the short term.

When we asked Jeff Bezos at a recent World Economic Forum why he didn't retire after launching Amazon, he dismissed the question impatiently as did 18 other billionaires I spoke to that week in Davos. From Oprah and Carlos Slim to Michael Bloomberg and Richard Branson, they all recoiled at the thought of retirement.

"I didn't get into this game to sit on a beach. Ha!" Bezos boomed with his signature guffaw and a roll of his eyes. "I pour my heart and soul into Amazon because it's changing the world for consumers, and we're only in day one of what we have to learn about how to serve people in this online world."

Not only are the greatest leaders eager to stay in the game long after they've become rich and successful, they're willing to risk their reputation to bring new and innovative ideas into the world. His shareholders were dismayed when Bezos refused to show a profit in the early years as he built a base for his business. They were alarmed when he decided to start manufacturing hand-held devices after many other firms had tried and failed miserably in the low margin consumer products business. But Bezos had a vision, and he was right. The Kindle has transformed the publishing business and the way we read. When it comes to launching a new product he believes in, Bezos is more interested in his long-term strategy than what critics have to say on launch day. If a new venture fits into his vision of Amazon's future, he'll gladly wait a handful of years or more for the payday that he knows will come.

ADMIRED

## What Doesn't Kill You Makes You Stronger

What other trade-offs does this tech leader make to stay true to Amazon's founding principles? Bezos told Fortune magazine, "Our culture is friendly and intense, but if push comes to shove we'll settle for intense." Amazon is built on what he calls a "culture of metrics." When his team is testing customer reaction to a website feature, data always decides the victor. While it is important to create a healthy and supportive working environment, Bezos would rather his employees feel focused on serving Amazon's biggest MVP: its customers.

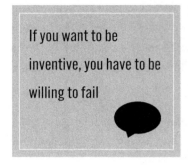

If you want to be inventive, you have to be willing to fail

Bezos knows not all of Amazon's ideas can be a hit, but failure today is another price he's willing to pay to come up with the next big thing tomorrow. "If you want to be inventive, you have to be willing to fail," he says. In Amazon's early days for example, they hired a staff of editors to write book and music reviews before scrapping the whole department in favor of customer-written reviews. They even made an unsuccessful attempt at auctions. However as long as he and his team can learn something useful from them, Bezos accepts missteps like these as a part of life.

## Ignore the "Second-Handers"

Marva Collins turned down two US Presidents when they offered her the job as Secretary of Education because she was too busy saving "hopeless" kids and sending them to college. Collins works with children on the streets who others have left behind, and those who do have parents in their lives, face issues like drug addiction, poverty, and gangs. But among the most difficult things these children deal with are people judging them. She says it's too easy to be seduced by other people's nasty, superficial judgments about us. Collins calls these people second-handers—critics who have a lot to say about others but don't do anything productive in their own lives.

"You have two kinds of people: the *creators* and the *second-handers*," Collins told us in an interview at PBS. "The *creator* is self-motivated, self-generated, and self-propelled. The *second-hander* is always trying to garner opinions of others and belongs to the crowd...they belong to the herd." The sad part is that these second-handers spend all their energy being against things, rather than investing that passion in creating value.

"We all want someone to lead us," says Collins. It's like in the *Wizard of Oz*, we are looking for a wizard. They go to the wizard seeking a heart, a brain, courage, and the wizard says you had these things. All you need to do is use it. When you get that great indomitable Self in your own belief, then all things are possible. You are going to make mistakes; don't beat yourself up for it. There is no such thing as failure. Failure is a place I rest, while I run the big race of success."

# Putting It to Work for You

So you are misunderstood. You know you're making progress when you start to get resistance.

What is the long-term value of what you or your MVP are trying to accomplish?

.................................................................................................................

.................................................................................................................

.................................................................................................................

How could you sell the long-term value to those that can be supportive of making that goal happen?

.................................................................................................................

.................................................................................................................

.................................................................................................................

.................................................................................................................

Who's support will you need and how could you sell them on providing that support?

.................................................................................................................

.................................................................................................................

.................................................................................................................

.................................................................................................................

# 12

## MEASURE

If goals are so great for your long-term success (and we strongly believe they are) then why do so many people not bother setting them and most fail to achieve them? Franklin-Covey found that over a third of their customers had given up on their New Year's resolutions by the end of January, and 77% had dropped out by the end of the year.

It doesn't have to be that way. In this section, we'll share critical ingredients that are essential to making goals work. Tool #9 reveals why it's so important to set goals that are meaningful to you and not just what you think you should strive for. Tool #10 offers help where you need it most—sticking with the daily and weekly tasks that lead to your goal.

## ADMIRED

Tool #11 is about building a feedback system to measure how well you're meeting your MVPs' needs.

# Tool #9: How to Sabotage Your Goals

There is a big difference between achieving goals for their own sake and setting objectives that are worth achieving. Goals can be frustrating. You likely know the feeling of having great intentions—this time you'll make the sales target, submit the monthly report on time, call mom every week, pursue that career change—which you just don't accomplish. The bad news is that most goals are subject to self-sabotage; the good news is you're not alone, and there's something you can do about it. There are four simple reasons why goals are so incredibly hard to achieve.

First, the brutal truth is that the goal does not matter to you enough to be worth the sacrifices necessary to achieve it. Most goals tend to be politically correct rather than personal or practical. If it's not your goal in the first place—and you haven't fully adopted it as your own—your body will reject it like a virus. Goals are too often an unnatural act designed to force you to do the admirable stuff that you "should" do rather than things you want to do or care about. No matter how good those goals may be for you or your company, you will resist them until they've become something that you accept as meaningful to you.

The second reason even meaningful new goals fail is because they compete with values that you hold even more dearly. New Year's resolutions are too often a game of wistful, wishful thinking. One year I (Mark) decided I would spend meaningful time with my family at least once a day, no matter how busy I was. We found that sharing dinnertime felt most natural, so the habit clicked. But when another goal—my new exercise and diet program—competed with that sacred family dinner, those new goals were doomed. Not only did the exercise time threaten a much more cherished supper with our daughter, the diet program also

# ADMIRED

attempted to force me to give up food that I liked. The new goals were robbing me of too many things in my life that I found more valuable.

## The Art of Goal Setting

It pays dividends to find the meaning behind each goal so you can imagine clever ways to support it. My goal to spend time with my spouse and daughter had found an ideal home, a natural place to fit in life and work. It was nicely associated with an enjoyable evening ritual around food and family. That's exactly the right recipe. But what could we do about my new goal to exercise? Rather than have a big meal together every night we decided to exercise as a family—do something physical— play basketball, take a hike or a dance class. This gave us a chance to bond in a different way rather than just be eating together.

And what about that diet? Rather than naively attempt to either quit our old lifestyle cold turkey or sacrifice the entire traditional meal, we transitioned to healthier eating habits by substituting a few healthy choices. We swapped sour cream with Greek yogurt. We substituted Ben & Jerry's Cherry Garcia frozen yogurt rather than something heavier. And then we discovered other dessert alternatives, like organic fruits. Nobody changes habit out of logic alone. Until I discovered that the organic stuff actually tasted better, it was not something I'd pay for or stick with because it violates other things that are valuable to me— things that are honestly (perhaps secretly) more important (like flavor!).

## Don't "Should" on Yourself

When was the last time you ordered a loved one or a coworker to make a major change in their life or work, and they just did it? I'm guessing

## MEASURE / TOOL #9: HOW TO SABOTAGE YOUR GOALS

never. When you dish out orders that your MVPs don't follow it's because they didn't see a good enough reason to change the status quo. It wasn't something they valued or cared about enough to make the necessary sacrifices.

If barking orders fails to motivate others, then why should you do any better with self-inflicted resolutions? We're asking ourselves to do something that we couldn't persuade others to do. Let's be honest, we resent and dread most goals in the first place because they ask us to give up things that we value. Stop punishing yourself. The purpose of goal setting is to achieve something you value—to live a more meaningful life.

Before you go about setting a new goal, spend some time thinking about what it is you really (really!) want. Think of these as pre-goals. They are the benefit you hope to receive (buying your dream home), NOT just the target (get out of debt). This may seem like a minor distinction, but to our minds and our motivation, it is a crucial one. We are much more willing to work hard and sacrifice when we know we'll receive a wonderful prize for our efforts. So when you set a goal, think about promising yourself a payday rather than just charging a tax.

Frame your goal around something valuable to you that you actually want. After all, you're not a very successful masochist. You probably don't respond well to shame, guilt, negative feelings, or making daily sacrifices for their own sake. That's because being the "biggest loser" (despite what the TV show leads us to believe) is far less appealing than *gaining* something desirable as a result. So what *do* you want? Is it to feel free in your own body again, more comfortable in your clothes, or to recapture the way you looked in younger years? If so, then picture yourself thin, fit, and happy.

ADMIRED

## Make a List...and Check it Twice

The third reason goals fail is because we obsess over how little we've accomplished rather than what needs to get done. In her book, *The Willpower Instinct*, Dr. Kelly McGonigal warns that when we focus on what we have accomplished, we tend to give up. By focusing on *why* we are doing something and what needs to get done, our willpower is strengthened.

Once you've gone through the pre-goal process, take some time to write down what you want to achieve: how does it look, how will you feel when you've achieved it, how will your life be different? Use all of your senses to make it as real as possible. Then prioritize it: where does this goal fit into other goals you may have? If it is near the top of the list you may need to reassess your other daily tasks to accommodate it. Set a due date for when you want or need to accomplish this goal. Create and schedule some new habits that will help you achieve the goal and then set checkpoints at which you'll look over your progress and decide what, if anything, you want to adjust.

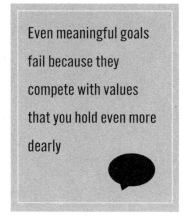

Even meaningful goals fail because they compete with values that you hold even more dearly

Cancer surgeon and bestselling author Atul Gawande talks about the radical effectiveness of a remarkably simple tool in his book *Checklist Manifesto*. At a time in human history when we have a vast amount of information at our fingertips we still, and often, fail to do what we set out to do. Gawande found that by following a simple checklist of essential steps, skilled practitioners of every stripe from surgeons to

## MEASURE / TOOL #9: HOW TO SABOTAGE YOUR GOALS

investors could avoid failures of ineptitude—not doing what they know very well how to do (like a doctor not washing his hands before surgery).

For our own purposes, making and following a checklist can be the link between setting a meaningful goal to achieving it. For those who have ever added an already-completed task to your to do list for the sheer thrill of crossing it off, the joy of the checklist is not new. What is new is making a religion of using it, not just when we feel a rush of organization coming on, but every day to achieve goals large and small.

## Never Give Up, and Other Myths About Goals

Setting value-based goals also allows you to do something that goal-setting books often consider failure: changing your mind. While checking items off your list is an effective tool, occasionally checking in with your dreams is also essential to achieving them. You may find that after weeks or months of sticking to your plan, your goal simply isn't possible. Something out of your control may have changed or maybe you learned more about how you really feel and decide your true goal lies down an avenue you didn't even know existed. It's so important to do this check-in every once in a while and look at both what you've learned and how you've grown. We're constantly changing and growing and our goals must do the same.

We sabotage our goals in seven ways:

**Myth #1: Stick to goals no matter what**

What we learned in our World Success Survey of high achievers is that successful people try and fail more often than the average population. Fearing failure, low achievers focus on taking fewer risks, resulting in less progress. They win less than high achievers. Quitting may be

# ADMIRED

unpleasant, but it's a great strategy when you discover you've set the wrong course. Letting go of a losing plan isn't failure; it's wisdom that you can use to set a better goal.

## Myth #2: Share your goals

This is great if you have super supportive, selfless friends. But sharing your dreams with all of the critics in your life can actually undermine your goals. Don't be afraid to keep your plan to yourself while you work out the kinks or until you feel more confident. You can always bring in the friends you know will have productive ideas and support. Share your values with them before stating the goal so they understand your motivation.

## Myth #3: Steel your emotions and blast through the goal

I read an article that recommended keeping your emotions out of goal setting. Emotions play a huge role in what we do on a day-to-day basis. Achieving goals is hard, and you'll need your emotions on your side to sustain the actions required to reach them. Aligning goals with what emotionally moves us is exactly what you need to turn them into achievements.

## Myth #4: Goals set too low have no challenge

I love low-challenge milestones because they are so attainable. They build confidence. The problem is not the level of challenge, but the level of meaning. If you don't care, it's not likely to happen. And if you accomplish something you don't care about, then how useful was that?

## Myth #5: Vague goals are useless

Yes it's hard to know when you've achieved a vague goal, but it's not impossible. When Steve Jobs was reinventing the smart phone—the changes he made were rather vague at first. It's often hard to be specific about something that has never existed before. What you must be clear about is what you value, and Jobs had a clear vision about changing things in ways that would make technology transparent, easier, more useful, and more seamless than traditional ways of doing things. But even he didn't predict all of the specs of the product that Apple eventually invented.

## Myth #6: Set realistic goals

Big Harry Audacious Goals can be very motivating to the right crowd. It wasn't realistic to think we could land on the moon, but we had faith that we could.

## Myth #7: Goals must be attainable

Life is too short to achieve every goal that others imagine for you. We have limited time and need to be judicial in the goals we set and assure they really matter to us. If your life was cut short by some tragedy on the way to a dream, would you look back to say the journey was worth it anyway?

ADMIRED

# Tool #10: Find Your Goal Buddy

So you've set some goals that really mean something to you and have a plan for achieving them. Great! Now comes the hard part: execution. To succeed, you'll need to make achieving your goal a deliberate practice— not only working on it every day but also reflecting on what's working, what's not, and making constant adjustments. But even working smart and hard on your goals won't matter unless you keep at it. That's why getting a daily reminder is essential to keeping up with your goals. And partnering with a goal buddy is one of the most important things you can do to achieve your goals and become more valuable to people who matter to you.

It is easy to become overwhelmed by the number of daily responsibilities we face. To give these new initiatives a fighting chance, you'll need a helper that shouts loud and clear over the noise of any particular day. For example, a friend of ours struggles to make exercise an everyday habit. She told us that when her husband asks her to go for a run with him in the morning it's all too easy for her to grumble some excuse about being too tired, roll over, and go back to sleep. She knows he'll still love her no matter how egregious her morning laziness. But when a close—and very sporty—friend recently asked to start exercising together, it was much harder for her to say no. She knew that Julie would take it personally if she made some lame excuse to skip their date. Julie took her exercise seriously, and as a new mom, she only had one chance in the day to do it. All of a sudden those early wake up calls were tolerable, and our friend would spring out of bed at 5:30, knowing Julie would be waiting for her. Her unwillingness to disappoint her friend, and the idea that she was somehow helping Julie meet *her* fitness goals, made it far easier for our friend to meet her own.

## MEASURE / TOOL #10: FIND YOUR GOAL BUDDY

The person you wake up next to every morning may seem like a natural choice, but sometimes it's easier to feel accountable to a stranger (someone who doesn't already love you in spite of your flaws) or even a piece of technology. Jawbone makes a wristband called UP that helps you track your activity throughout the day and night and allows you to set alerts. UP will vibrate to remind you to wake you up or exercise. It also comes with a built-in online community whose members you can interact and compete with. Nike makes a similar product called the FuelBand. GoalBuddy.com is an online tool that lets you set goals that are SMART (specific, measurable, attainable, relevant, and time-bound), connects you with others with similar goals who can encourage you, and supports you with reminders and incentives along the way. And don't overlook the virtues of the good old index card system. As long as you get into the habit of referring to them every day, simple reminders written on a 3x5 index card can be as effective as any high tech tool.

Getting a daily reminder is essential to keeping up with your goals

## Follow-Up: The Difference between Success & Failure

Bestselling author and leadership expert Marshall Goldsmith and Howard Morgan conducted a study of 86,000 thousands of leaders to find out what leadership training actually improved leaders. Regardless of the training method they used—classroom, coaching, onsite training, on-the-job coaching—the factor that gave the greatest return was follow-up. The leaders who received consistent follow-up from their co-workers or other MVPs achieved their goals. Those whose co-workers or friends did little to no follow up, largely lost interest, got busy with life, and did not achieve the goals they set. The difference was a vast

**ADMIRED**

change in leadership effectiveness.

The results of this study showed that just the fact that someone bugged them about their goals is more important than the expertise of the person who is giving the nudge. This is perhaps one of the best endorsements for getting a coach, although it may be disheartening to coaches who think their success is largely due to their unique talents. The study was led by someone whose feelings would be hard to hurt in that regard. Goldsmith's expertise was once again validated in 2011 when he was voted the number one leadership thinker in the world by *Harvard Business Review*. He and Howard Morgan discuss this research for an article they wrote called "Leadership is a Contact Sport" for the journal *Strategy+Business*, which eventually named it one of the nine most impactful articles of the year.

Goldsmith and Morgan also believe that the key variable is personal ownership of the goal. The leaders all received training, but the difference in results boiled down to what they did on their own, after the program. The individuals who improved set clear, meaningful goals, shared these goals with others, and accepted their help and support. They also made the time and put in the effort to get ongoing follow-up and positive reinforcement.

## Remind Yourself Why

Have you been taking consistent action toward your goal? If you answered yes, researchers at Hong Kong University of Science and the University of Chicago say you are 70% more likely to slack off when given the opportunity to take action toward your goal today. Psychologists call this moral licensing. We reward our good behavior with bad behavior. But this does not mean we are all doomed to fail. The secret lies in what we say to ourselves when we make progress.

When researchers have students tell them why they wanted to achieve the goal, only 31% went on to engage in behavior counter to their goal. When we focus on what matters about our goal—I'm working out everyday so I can play with my kids—rather than how good we are, we are more likely to achieve it. Set up constant reminders, not only to *do* the necessary tasks, but also to tell yourself *why* you set the goals in the first place.

# ADMIRED

## 💡 Deliberate Practice

Professor K. Anders Ericsson of the Florida State University came across a concept he calls deliberate practice while observing world-class professionals at work and determining successful behaviors. The first part of this research found that nobody becomes great without work. There are no examples of high-level performance without experience and practice. The study also showed that world-class performers take a minimum of ten years of practice to become, well, world-class.

Deliberate practice is a structured way of practicing the skills necessary to achieve your goal.

Decide to practice X number of times per week

Observe the results of each practice trail

Make appropriate adjustments to get better

Then practice for several hours everyday (including weekends)

Steps two and three are critical because practice makes permanent, not perfect. So if you don't take the time to correct yourself after each practice session you will be making your mistakes permanent. Goals may change as our circumstances change but the values underlying our goals are more constant. Set meaningful, value-centric markers with your team so you can change your goal as you learn from each trail run.

MEASURE / TOOL #10: FIND YOUR GOAL BUDDY

# Putting It to Work for You

Who could be your mastermind group or person?

.......................................................................................................................

.......................................................................................................................

What tools would be useful – checklist, 3x5 card system, email, phone call, text, robot?

.......................................................................................................................

.......................................................................................................................

What prizes or special recognition could your goal buddies give you to make your victories public?

.......................................................................................................................

.......................................................................................................................

ADMIRED

# Tool #11: Feed Forward, Not Backward

Jack Welch slumped in his chair, wringing his hands as he told Mark about one of the most stressful jobs he had performed in his celebrated career. "I knew damn well I didn't want to keep doing that job. And I only lasted for three weeks. Because I couldn't take it." Welch had accepted a job drilling holes in corks at a cork factory. "I drilled the hole and threw the final product in the barrel, and every time I got the bottom of the barrel almost covered the supervisor would come along and empty it." He never got the satisfaction of seeing his objective achieved—after all his painstaking effort. The lack of clear positive feedback drove him nuts. "Oh, God, it was the worst job you can imagine."

It's stressful to work without knowing whether we are making a meaningful impact. It's particularly unsettling if the feedback is not clear or you don't understand how to use it to improve your performance. We've all been victims of MVPs who rant about a mistake or mishap without giving you the tools or insights to do better next time. There is an art to giving and getting feedback. What we all want is a way to succeed. This is why leading executive coach Marshall Goldsmith recommends giving feed *forward* rather than feedback. Feed forward means giving people the news they can use *before* they take action, rather than bemoaning the past without offering a solution.

How can you set up a system for getting more feed forward about what your MVPs value? Here are four key elements:

**Get feedback as soon after the action as possible.** While asking your MVPs to complete daily surveys is impractical, monthly feedback systems are not responsive enough to change performance levels. Feedback systems that are easy for your MVP to use provide the best compromise between daily harassment and a long delay. Managers can be on the look out for the behaviors they want and give a thumbs-up when they see them. They could give a spot award or send an email recognizing a team member for doing something great for a client or a coworker. Customers can be given smile and frown icons that they drop into a fishbowl after each encounter.

**Be specific about actions and behaviors rather than people and personalities.** When giving feedback or setting up a feedback system, be very clear what the desired action or behavior is. Specifically what did you do that they liked or didn't like? Recognition and incentive programs that acknowledge people rather than actions can be more de-motivating than motivating. When you create Employee of the Month programs to recognize one person the rest of your team will think "why him and not me?" unless there is a clear measure for performance. It's better to have an Achievement of the Week with a case history about how Maggie pulled off this amazing accomplishment rather than simply posting her smiling photo—which leaves the perception that she mysteriously is the manager's favorite. Programs that have measurable targets are best, so the team can aspire to those measures rather than a personality contest.

> Feed forward means giving people the news they can use *before* they take action, rather than bemoaning the past without offering a solution.

**Tie actions to the overarching mission.** In other words, connect the dots for people so that it's clear how every step or milestone in the process contributes to the overall outcome you're seeking. Explain why each action is important. Explain why it is important to the group's

## ADMIRED

mission. Say how well they performed the action in light of the mission. Tell them what impact they've had.

**Discuss next steps.** Small wins are important to celebrate. Every feedback system is improved with milestone celebrating and marking constructive progress along the way.

If you get negative feedback, determine how you could get better on the next try. There is nothing worse than asking for feedback and then not responding to it. Brainstorm on the next steps. Do you need more information, a new skill, additional contacts? Then try again. How can you make the reporting of the goal more immediate? How can you give rapid feedback more quickly regarding how your employees and customers are doing? How can each participant do the reporting and get immediate feedback regarding where they stand?

MEASURE / TOOL #11: FEED FORWARD, NOT BACKWARD

# Putting It To Work for You

How could you get feedback ASAP for really important goals?

..........................................................................................................

..........................................................................................................

How could you get feedback on what specific actions worked or didn't work?

..........................................................................................................

..........................................................................................................

..........................................................................................................

How could you recognize those who support you in achieving your goals?

..........................................................................................................

..........................................................................................................

..........................................................................................................

..........................................................................................................

..........................................................................................................

If you would like someone to change, how could you tell them what you want them to do and then encourage the change that happens?

..........................................................................................................

..........................................................................................................

..........................................................................................................

150

# 13

## INCENTIVES

To be admired, respected, and valued for what you do, you'll need to give the people who matter most to you the right incentives—something they value so much that they will appreciate your skills and contribution. One of the best ways to do that is to give your MVPs the tools and support to express themselves more creatively and a way to participate in and "own" the goals that you've set for them. For example, Tool #12 shows how fast-growing social media companies provide an artistic canvas for their MVPs—a platform for their customers to create something they believe has great personal value. Tool #13 stresses the importance of

# ADMIRED

finding out what motivates your MVPs and how you can leverage their passion to meet your shared goals. Tool #14 helps you unearth what your MVP really values.

# Tool #12: Help Them Invent It

The wave heading for them was so huge and fierce that it tossed cars and homes like toys as it wiped out neighborhood after neighborhood. A child wept, clinging to a dollhouse, as the rushing flood swept her away. Thousands were drowned or crushed in minutes. Over 15,000 lives were lost and millions couldn't go home. And it all happened in the heart of one of the world's greatest technological superpowers.

After the devastating earthquake and tsunami that hit Japan, one woman made a global plea for support in the most unusual way. She begged people all over the world to record their own personal version of the song "Lean on Me" and post it where it could be heard using the hot new GLEE music app from a popular startup called Smule.

Within moments, she had incited the largest global impromptu virtual choir in recording history. She inspired thousands of customers, young and old from 140 nations to make their own soulful statement in a profoundly unique way at this time when most people felt otherwise helpless to contribute. Each individual crooned into their cell phones, joining others asynchronously, then hearing their contribution reformatted to blend with the rest of this enormous group. The overwhelming majority of these Smule customers didn't know each other, so this was a choir of like-minded strangers who chose to collaborate without prior planning, meeting, or permission, and with no group of lawyers to draw up a music contract.

The Smule app displays on your smartphone screen, an image of Earth spinning in space. You see bright white streams of light rising from all over the planet, each beam representing an individual singing their heart out. As you touch the screen and turn the globe with your finger,

**ADMIRED**

you can roll over every inch of the world to hear each lightbeam perform—individuals singing their song. This is one of a dozen Smule vocal and instrumental apps—from pianos and guitars to the ancient Ocarina flute.

## Empowering Creativity

Using this app, anyone can make their own creative impact without delay or auditions. You can instantly become a musician or vocalist without the skills or talent once required. You can create your songs spontaneously, hear your attempts auto-tuned so they sound right, then combine them with others and even add harmony to the background music of your choice. And most important, you can share your song and engage with others as if it was entirely your own original work of art (because it pretty much is!) One year after the tsunami, nearly 4,000 singers have added their voices to "Lean on Me" (www.smule.com/japantribute), and altogether, the chorus of voices has been singing for more than 180 hours.

This has been a very personal and emotional mission for the two Palo Alto-based Smule founders. Ge Wang is a Stanford professor in computer music raised in China and Jeff Smith is a veteran CEO raised in Salt Lake City who has launched and listed Nasdaq startups (and is now a Stanford PhD candidate in computer music). These inventors see their business model as more social movement than social media. It's a *cause* for them, a manifesto for creative freedom. Music bridges politics and deeply held differences that otherwise hold people apart. Music has a visceral impact on our hearts, opening our willingness to replace sadness with joy in the worst of circumstances. Wang, Smith, and their burgeoning creative team believe every human being deserves the right to express themselves musically—despite individual skill and talent—because making music together runs deep in every society in human history since the beginning of time. In the few years since Wang and Smith started this little company, their customers have performed more than 600 million songs around the world.

Despite having participated in music in high school, there's nothing remotely hip about your authors, Mark and Bonita. So when we first heard about this wild idea from cofounder Jeff Smith, (one of Mark's coaching clients from Jeff's prior successful Nasdaq company), it was easy for us to become founding investors. The bottom line is irresistible: People will admire your services—and happily evangelize them—when you make it easy for them to express themselves creatively. From Facebook to YouTube, when users can show the world that they're doing something they value, they can't wait to share it with others. When your customer uses your product or service to say, "*I've created this—this is my own contribution,*" then you've won their loyalty.

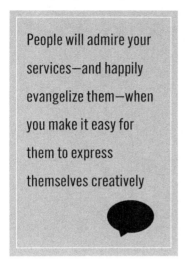

People will admire your services—and happily evangelize them—when you make it easy for them to express themselves creatively

Prerna Gupta and Parag Chordia, educated at Yale and Stanford, joined Smule with their own startup, Khush, following a similar vision. Among myriad apps, they can help you turn any tone-deaf spoken sentence into music and even convert your words into rap automatically. From LinkedIn, FaceBook, and YouTube, to Google, Flickr, and even Home Depot—successful companies understand that when they facilitate their customers' creative ability to build something that matters, everyone wins.

ADMIRED

## Help Your MVPs Own Your Inventions

This is the mantra for social media in the 21st century—getting your customers to identify with your products or services so much that they feel they own them. And it is another tool you can use to empower your MVPs and garner their admiration. Giving them the power to make their own imprint and share the results with others makes your MVP an even greater advocate for your work in the marketplace.

## INCENTIVES / TOOL #12: HELP THEM INVENT IT

### Who Do You Think You Are?

In our interviews with high achievers we've consistently noticed that successful people identify with their objectives and goals rather than with their challenges or flaws. They talk about having health challenges, but don't call themselves sick. They describe going through difficult financial circumstances, but don't say they were poor. They failed but they were not failures. Their choice of words is clear. They don't just work toward their goal; they are crusaders. When we identify with the solution, we can make amazing progress.

High achievers create a *role* to go with their goal. In other words, when your job description is also your self-description—your identity—then you're not in conflict between what you're supposed to be doing in the office and what you really want to be doing with your life and work. When you're in alignment you hold nothing back. Ladies and gentlemen, you're off to the races.

The same is true when your customer identifies themselves with your product. Adam Prewett of Playdom, a videogaming company, said that when your customer begins saying, "I'm a gamer"—instead of simply "I play games"—they are more likely to purchase products. When your customer feels that their avatar is personal—that it's a representation of who they are or want to be—they are more likely to purchase clothing to make their avatar look hot.

ADMIRED

# Putting it to work for you

How can your MVPs own what you are creating?

..........................................................................................................

..........................................................................................................

When you describe yourself to others what do you tell them? Are you associating yourself with attributes you want to be known for?

..........................................................................................................

..........................................................................................................

..........................................................................................................

..........................................................................................................

..........................................................................................................

# Tool #13: What's It Worth to Them

Susan's company had set goals three years in a row and missed them every time. The team agreed these were critical goals and yet they failed to make them happen. Susan is a talented, organized, and efficient operations manager for a publishing company. Feeling frustrated she asked us to sit in on one of her staff meetings to help figure out what's going wrong. Her staff was dedicated, passion-driven, and capable. Yet when we compared their individual motivations with the company's goals, it was easy to see why certain goals didn't move forward.

For example, the team knew they needed to create technical documentation for the product, but no one enjoyed writing procedures that became outdated faster than they were written. So they didn't get done. Now, Susan could punish people who didn't make the deadline, or as we suggested, we could find someone on the team who might enjoy the task, and not only get it done, but do it extraordinarily well. It turns out there was one manager who loved video production and editing. When we suggested that company create the procedures as video clips, she grabbed the project and it was done in a flash. In many cases, when you can change the goals just enough to fit the internal motivations, passions, and talents of the team, you can accelerate progress toward meeting your organizational goals, and do it with greater creativity and quality.

In a follow-up call with Susan, she reported, "profits were up 300% in an industry that was down overall. And for the first time in the company's history we achieved all our goals and I've never worked on a more supportive team."

## ADMIRED

Each of us is motivated differently. We have preferences for how we like to work and the rewards that matter to us. Learning these things about each person supporting us is critical to be an effective leader and motivator. It's better to connect to something that already motivates people and put that to work. Knowing what grabs your team's attention will help them drive projects home faster and better than even they imagined.

## Unintended Consequences

I (Mark) was in a hurry and pulled into a fast-food drive-through. After placing the order and paying for my meal, the clerk asked that I pull into the street and park and they would walk my meal out to me. The curiosity overwhelmed me and I asked why I was waiting in the street for my meal. They said they were paid based on how fast they got me through the line. There is nothing wrong with speed, but when the restaurant set that objective they needed to watch how creatively it was implemented so that they could reward what was working and avoid the unintended consequence of people gaming the system.

> It's better to connect to something that already motivates people and put that to work.

Incentive programs are very powerful for changing behavior but you have to be careful what you wish for. It's tricky to measure all the factors that equal customer satisfaction or a happy family. Ironically, some of the best incentive plans involve observing what is already motivating individuals and finding clever ways to incorporate them in achieving your goals.

## INCENTIVES / TOOL #13: WHAT'S IT WORTH TO THEM

### Give People Status

From the beginning of time humans have moved mountains to achieve status in their communities. In the Mayan cultures, status was achieved by being selected for execution and honorees gladly accepted. You can tell a lot about a culture by what things it places in high esteem—athletic ability, physical beauty, or level of education. We may confer high status on the person with the fastest turn around time, the most published papers, or even the most spiritual.

Take a conscious look at what you value, what's really important. Can you create a ritual to give status to people who give you that? From Kindergarten graduations to the Nobel Prize ceremonies, rituals play a profound role in keeping us focused on what is right in our lives.

Create an award that symbolizes how your MVPs have invested time and effort. You will send a powerful message to everyone when you create ritual around what you value. People are keenly tuned to things that will give them a sense of importance. We gravitate toward communities that make us feel significant.

What behaviors do you want to encourage in others and how can you give them status for that?

ADMIRED

# Putting it to work for you

What are the things that motivate each team member or support person?

.................................................................................................................

.................................................................................................................

.................................................................................................................

.................................................................................................................

.................................................................................................................

How can you incorporate what they love into their work?

.................................................................................................................

.................................................................................................................

.................................................................................................................

.................................................................................................................

.................................................................................................................

## INCENTIVES / TOOL #13: WHAT'S IT WORTH TO THEM

How can you give status to others for what is important to you?

What behaviors do you want to encourage in others and how can you give them status for that?

ADMIRED

# Tool #14: Know What Your MVP Values

The last thing Ivan remembered about the desert was the explosion—the heat, the noise, the pain. "I can't believe I was taken down by a damn IED," he thought, utterly frustrated and ashamed. He couldn't stop thinking about that day, probably his last as a lieutenant in the US Army, and what it had made him: useless. Ivan was blind—an almost unbearable reality—yet his doctors and nurses seemed determined to torture him some more. They wanted him out of bed, walking, doing physical therapy, talking to someone. What they didn't seem to understand was that Ivan wasn't going anywhere ever again. He obviously couldn't go back to being a Ranger, so what was the use? But the woman who walked into his hospital room next had different plans.

General Gale Pollack has spent her career helping and serving others, first as an army nurse and eventually as surgeon general of the United States Armed Forces. When she walked into Ivan's hospital room in Bethesda, Maryland, that day she hoped she could find some hook to bring him back to the land of the living. She didn't know what to expect from the wounded soldier lying in that bed. So she started from the beginning. When the lieutenant told Pollack that he was blind she remembers that he looked like a deflating balloon, like he was letting go of his life energy. He didn't mention his other injuries; he focused solely on the blindness and his certainty that it had ruined his life. "All I've ever wanted to do was be in the army," he told her, "and now I can't."

> General Pollack had done something crucial for Ivan: she found out what he wanted—what motivated him.

## INCENTIVES / TOOL #14: KNOW WHAT YOUR MVP VALUES

Searching for what he really valued, the general asked what Ivan liked so much about military life. At this he suddenly became animated, recounting stories from his days as a Ranger. Pollack interrupted him, "I think you're lying to me," she said curtly. "You can't be a Ranger because Rangers aren't quitters. So you'd better stop telling people you're a Ranger. You're an embarrassment because you're a quitter."

Now the lieutenant was mad. And when he rolled over in bed and yelled, He was blind, hadn't she heard him?, Pollack made her final move. She shouted right back, "I've got other blind service members in the army so what the hell's your problem?" Ivan went silent, stunned by what he had heard. "Maam," he said. "Nobody told me I could stay in the army." With that she knew she had his attention, and so she gave him the name of another recently blinded soldier who was back at work. Her final message to the lieutenant that day was that if he wanted to be in the army then his goal was to get well and stay focused.

## Investigate, Don't Assume

"You're a quitter." These are strong words for anyone to hear, much less someone at a physical and emotional crossroads. But General Pollack had done something crucial for Ivan: she found out what he wanted—what motivated him. Though she had served in the military for years and had seen a lifetime of wounded soldiers, she didn't assume she knew what Ivan thought or felt. And, after years of doling out tough love, she didn't assume she knew what would motivate him. Instead she investigated. Ivan's frustration and (incorrect) assumption that he would have to leave the service was evident. But by asking him to tell her what he liked about being a Ranger, she was able to learn what he valued most. She found the most essential driver of success for Ivan and pushed. She saw where this young man really wanted to be and used it

## ADMIRED

to get his attention and plant the seed of motivation.

Quite naturally, humans view the world from inside our own bubble. We behave like goldfish swimming around glass bowls clearly seeing our thoughts, dreams, and values, but not looking out to see what others value. It's difficult to know what is important to someone else, and doing it consistently can take some practice. Take the time to peer inside another person's bubble. Observing and understanding what's valuable to the MVPs in your life is a crucial step in being more valuable to them.

## INCENTIVES / TOOL #14: KNOW WHAT YOUR MVP VALUES

### 💡 Keep It Simple & Beautiful

Apple is the world's most admired company, according to Fortune Magazine, and the most valuable, as measured by its stock price. Companies the world over are clamoring to understand how Apple can make its products look and feel like it's worth two times more than competitors' and convince us all to line up around the block to buy it. The secret is in creating simple, intuitive products in a glamorously beautiful package. Steve Jobs introduced every Apple product individually, as a breakthrough, like unique pieces of art.

When Steve Jobs borrowed my (Mark's) Rio mp3 player at a business lunch in 2000, I was a chairman of Rioport. We were hot at the time, selling almost a quarter million digital music devices before the iPod was invented. He did me a brutal, unintentional favor that changed my life. Jobs handed back my mp3 player, giggling, and told me it was a geeky piece of crap.

I could have been insulted (we loved the Rio and so did a million other people). Instead I avoided the personal disaster that would have come from investing my savings in Rioport at that point in history. A year later Jobs introduced the iPod and iTunes, charging 99 cents a song during the time of Napster. The iPod had far fewer features than our Rio player, but that was part of Apple's magic. The iPod was easier to navigate, it also looked more expensive and cool, but most important, unlike Rio, it required zero technical knowledge to work with other devices.

Apple didn't invent the PC, the smartphone, the graphical user interface or the digital music player, but Jobs still reinvented all those industries. He brought brilliant industrial design to clunky technological objects, transforming them from nerdy gadgets into fashion statements. Then he tied them all together so they'd work without a degree in electrical engineering. The story you tell—the package you create with the service and the product—must be as simple, intuitive, and beautiful to your MVPs as the content. The iPod strutted like another supermodel in Apple's stable, working seamlessly with the entire Apple universe, making it practical and easy to use; not just another pretty face.

ADMIRED

# Putting It to Work for You:

Observe your MVP. Is what they want and what they do in alignment?

.................................................................................................................

.................................................................................................................

What actions could you take to help them get more of what they want?

.................................................................................................................

.................................................................................................................

.................................................................................................................

.................................................................................................................

.................................................................................................................

When your MVP is upset, what are they telling you they want?

.................................................................................................................

.................................................................................................................

.................................................................................................................

.................................................................................................................

.................................................................................................................

# 14

## RECRUIT

Whether you're seeking new customers or team members, or rallying your current MVPs around a new idea or product, recruiting is a crucial strategy in an admired leader's arsenal. Tool #15 stresses the importance of surrounding yourself with people whose skills complement your own and fill in the weak spots. Tool #16 will free you from the drudgery of networking and reveal a more powerful approach to recruiting a strong support system. Tool #17 is about preparing your MVPs to face challenges on their own. And tool #18 will explain why getting sucked into the blame game not only destroys trust, but squanders a golden opportunity to innovate.

# Tool #15: Hire Your Weakness

Nobody gets anything worthwhile done alone. Anyone who is respected, valued, and admired achieves success only with the support and expertise of a great team. Sharing power and relying on others (especially when you think you could do it better) are often the most difficult skills for an entrepreneur to learn. But it's the only way to grow a successful organization. No one does it alone.

Billionaire Charles Schwab believes his dyslexia gave him the humility and discipline necessary to build and rely on a team. For Schwab, it was an essential secret to his success in transforming the financial services industry. I (Mark) will never forget the sweltering May afternoon when Schwab reluctantly approached the podium at the Annual Meeting of Stockholders for the newly listed public company, The Charles Schwab Corporation. It was an extraordinarily hot day in San Francisco, and all the men in suits had sweated through their shirts. My stomach was in knots, and I would soon discover that Chuck was even more nervous than I.

> When someone is admired, it's not always obvious how often or artfully those high achievers ask for help and depend on it to be successful.

As his communications chief, I had carefully prepared a cleanly typed script, but it turned to gibberish as he glanced down at it. We shared a moment of surprise as we noticed the paper trembling in my hands, and then Schwab sighed and tilted his head, as if inviting me to replace him on stage in the imposing Grand Ballroom where over a thousand stockholders had gathered. It was an intimidating setting for two introverts. Schwab squinted at the page trying to make some sense of the two-page keynote. The company had just come through some hard times and rocky markets, and we thought the crowd might not be entirely friendly.

## The Gift of Imperfection

For many years, Schwab feared that his nerves might reveal a disability that he had never before talked about in public. After all, he wondered how reassuring it would be to his stockholders and customers to know that their famous investment advisor—the expert they were trusting with their retirement money—didn't just dread public speaking, but had nearly been expelled from college after failing his language classes, including English. No matter how gifted he was in finance and customer service, Schwab is dyslexic and reading anything had always been extraordinarily difficult. Any attempts to recite a note in public or read from a teleprompter required heroic effort.

In Schwab's case, the very same "weakness" that undermines many promising academic and professional careers turned out to be a source of genius for him, just as it has been for other innovators with so-called learning disabilities—Albert Einstein, Walt Disney, Richard Branson, George Washington, John Chambers and even Agatha Christie. Like many gifted entrepreneurs, Schwab developed coping mechanisms like asking for support from coworkers and employees. This habit made him a better leader, as it forced him to build a supportive team that he truly relied on and appreciated.

**ADMIRED**

## Turn Your Wounds into Wisdom

When someone is admired, it's not always obvious how often or artfully those high achievers ask for help and depend on it to be successful. In many ways, leaders turn their flaws and wounds into wisdom. When you know you're not a wizard in every subject, you're more likely to recruit others who have those great talents and skills. That's the best trait any leader or entrepreneur can develop early in his or her career.

"In some respects, the positive side of this learning issue was probably my early recognition that I wasn't strong in every component—reading, writing and all those kinds of things," says Schwab. You have to have the courage to face the reality that no one is an expert at everything, and you could not grow a business alone even if you were Superman. "I knew I needed to have other people who could complement me in different parts of the business that I was developing."

While most dyslexics have trouble reading books, many develop a skill for reading people. One reason is because they have the humility to ask questions and pay attention to what people do rather than make assumptions. Out of habit and genuine interest, Schwab peered deeply into the hearts and minds of his customers unlike any other financial services firm at the time. Based on what he learned from them, Schwab created ways for average consumers to invest that were so blindingly simple that tens of millions of consumers couldn't resist its appeal.

The downfall of many brilliant entrepreneurs is believing their ideas and skills are all they need to build a great company. At our Venture Lab at Stanford University, we quickly realized that entrepreneurs' arrogance was one of the major factors in why nine out of ten ventures fail. Too many leaders lose their footing before they learn that they must recruit a capable team with expertise in many areas in order to execute and expand their vision.

## RECRUIT / TOOL #15: HIRE YOUR WEAKNESS

Because Schwab had learned this lesson early in life, he began developing and engaging an unbeatable team from day one. Schwab says, "I have been able to recognize my strengths and my deficits and build up around me a team of great people in the areas of deficit," he says. "I think that probably has been the single most important benefit that I received from having this learning issue early on in my life."

## Sara Blakely Hires Her Weakness

Billionaire Sara Blakely had a similar ambition. She could not wait to replace herself in all the key roles of her company as fast as she possibly could. "As soon as I could, I hired my weakness!" Blakely is the founder of the groundbreaking undergarment brand Spanx, and she's the company's heart and soul, but not its CEO. In the beginning, Blakely *was* every department from packing and shipping to "before and after" model (she made poster-size photos of her own tush to flaunt the benefits of Spanx).

She quickly learned what parts of the business she did and didn't enjoy and, more importantly, which she was good at. Then as soon as she could afford to hire her weaknesses, she did. Spanx CEO Laurie Ann Goldman joined the team about two years in, allowing Blakely to focus on areas where she can add the most value. Blakely is a natural in business, having realized without training that running, operating, and growing a business year after year requires a very different skill set than starting one. This can be a hard realization for many managers because it requires both humility, and the driving ambition to make your company succeed. The job of a leader is to recruit and develop other leaders. It's the only way for your organization to become free and capable enough to grow.

## ADMIRED

That's been Blakely's secret. She started the company with $5,000 in her savings account and a strong belief in her idea. When Oprah named Spanx one of her "favorite things", the sudden popularity created an avalanche of new business and Blakely had only quit her job selling fax machines two weeks before. After twelve years, a lot of work, and some very big breaks, she has built a billion-dollar undergarment empire.

With no formal business training, Blakely didn't start with much, but what she had in spades was passion for her product and a lot of resourcefulness. With a talent for recruiting great people, she has managed to build her brand without advertising, incurring no debt, and using no outside investors. For Blakely, this rare combination of confidence and willingness to empower people in key roles has made her business a huge success.

RECRUIT / TOOL #15: HIRE YOUR WEAKNESS

# Putting It to Work for You

What tasks can you delegate?

......................................................................................................

......................................................................................................

......................................................................................................

How can you help someone else develop a skill so they could help you?

......................................................................................................

......................................................................................................

......................................................................................................

Who could you partner with who would love to do what is necessary to get the job done?

......................................................................................................

......................................................................................................

......................................................................................................

Set a timetable for building a team to support you.

......................................................................................................

......................................................................................................

......................................................................................................

ADMIRED

# Tool #16: Stop Networking

I hate networking books because the advice often feels so manipulative, mercenary, and self-serving. And who really has time for all of that schmoozing when we're so busy at work already? But in most professions, building and maintaining a strong and stimulating community is critically important to becoming more valuable and recognized in your field.

What we used to call networking—developing short term contacts intended to meet your momentary needs and ambitions—you should consider relationship management or community building. The key is to shift from transactional relationships to meaningful ones based on common interests and objectives. This can be essential to finding out what's happening in your industry and learning best practices and new ways of developing business. When you're looking to find a new job or to get promoted, that's usually when most people realize they need to be networking. It can be really helpful to compare notes with peers and get the support of new friends you've met in your field.

The best way to get valuable support from others is to add value first— to offer help, referrals, ideas, and introductions for others as best you can. But it doesn't have to be the daunting task it may seem to be or require attending endless events with a room full of strangers. At many professional associations, there are new membership volunteers assigned to show you the ropes. We're often surprised how quickly you can put yourself in a position of leadership in these organizations. Most professional and alumni organizations are hungry for help and welcome most anyone willing to volunteer to manage or do work for the meetings. With a little extra time and effort, you will be invited to join the board for an event or for the group, and in so doing have the opportunity to deepen or expand your community and visibility.

## Build Your Community

For more than 40 years, my (Mark's) fellow Stanford alum Bob King and his wife Dottie have hosted exchange students in their home. They have found that many of these bright young people are a wealth of insights, international contacts, and well, treasure!

One home stay student introduced Bob to his friend Eric Xu who had joined Internet engineer Robin Li to launch a Chinese-language search engine. Bob, an investment partner at Peninsula Capital in Menlo Park, California, provided seed funding. He and Dottie were on hand in 2005 when the company, Baidu, made its debut on NASDAQ. Today, it has a market capitalization of $50 billion and employs more than 10,000 people in China. Now that's some network. The Kings were able to commit $150 million to Stanford's new entrepreneurship center that fights poverty around the world. The gift is the biggest in Stanford's history (and extraordinary by global standards) and was just part of the winnings that came from one student home stay.

Another one of the Kings' home stay students, Andreata Muforo, Stanford MBA '09 from Zimbabwe, brought peers from her global study trip in Africa to their home for dinner. "We heard how those first-hand experiences compelled some of the MBAs to return for internships in Africa," said Dottie. "We saw the direct connection between the learning experience and the motivation to make change." Bob adds, "We believe that innovation and entrepreneurship are the engines of growth to lift people out of poverty

## More Isn't Better

Strive for quality in your networking, not quantity. Networking can be overwhelming if you try to amass a certain number of people. Instead, select a few people to be in your network and invest in them. It's important to choose people who care about the same things you care about. First, do an inventory of your current network. Make a list of the people you trust and assess your relationship. Are you spending the time necessary to keep in touch with this MVP? Could you be devoting more attention to the relationship? Is there someone new who you'd like to have a quality connection with, but haven't put any time into that yet?

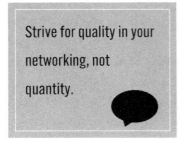

Once you've identified the people you'd like in your network, think about how you can help them with their goals. Strive for a reciprocal relationship that both nurtures your needs and your MVP's. When you are invited to a special event in your field, think about which person in your network would benefit from attending and invite them along. When you focus on being more valuable to your network of MVPs, the natural result is more value flows back to you. Get into a habit of cultivating your relationships monthly. You'll be surprised how satisfying it is to invest in and reap the many benefits of a high-quality network.

RECRUIT / TOOL #16: STOP NETWORKING

# Putting It to Work for You

What are the roles that could help you achieve your goals?

.................................................................................................................

.................................................................................................................

.................................................................................................................

.................................................................................................................

.................................................................................................................

Who are main 10 to 12 people who could help you with each of your goals? Make a list of how you could improve your relationship with them?

.................................................................................................................

.................................................................................................................

.................................................................................................................

.................................................................................................................

.................................................................................................................

.................................................................................................................

.................................................................................................................

.................................................................................................................

.................................................................................................................

## ADMIRED

What professional organizations should you be part of?

.................................................................................................

.................................................................................................

What non-profits contribute to your passions and professional interests? How could you help those non-profits?

.................................................................................................

.................................................................................................

Where do your goals and these key people's goals overlap?

.................................................................................................

.................................................................................................

.................................................................................................

.................................................................................................

How could you help them with their goals?

.................................................................................................

.................................................................................................

.................................................................................................

.................................................................................................

.................................................................................................

# Tool #17: Get Someone Ready

Is your team ready to take the wheel? If you're the only one who can drive your ambitions—at home and at work—you're in trouble.

It had been a school day like any other for the kids in Milton, Washington. That is until their bus driver started gasping for breath and then fainted behind the wheel. The kids were terrified. There are no seatbelts, airbags, or rollbars to protect children if a school bus swings out of control. There is no co-pilot, no other licensed driver aboard to take the wheel in an emergency. So one teenager did the unthinkable: he leapt to the wheel and calmly steered the bus to the side of the road. The kids administered CPR to the driver until the paramedics arrived and rushed him to the hospital. Afterward, thirteen-year-old Jeremy Wuitschick said of course he had been very scared. But somehow he was still able to safely park the bus and turn off the engine while his fellow students dialed 911.

How many seventh graders—or adults—would have the temerity and skill to do that? How had he developed the sense of caring or confidence to want to try? Why was this kid so capable in the face of real danger? Doing what Jeremy was able to do that day is rarely just instinctive. It's tempting to imagine that we could be "a natural" at the new things we attempt, particularly in a crisis. The truth is that confidence and skill come with practice.

## Practice Makes Prepared

As a seventh grader, Jeremy would not normally have even touched a steering wheel for a few years. But because he had always shown an

## ADMIRED

interest, his mom had begun having him move the car up and down the driveway as a reward for washing it. This may seem like a minor thing, but what she was doing for Jeremy was significant in developing him as a leader. She trusted him behind the wheel—a big deal, particularly for someone his age—and that built Jeremy's confidence. His mom respected his potential ability to take on an important adult task, and equally important, he knew she supported his interest in driving a car. Showing respect for something he values is no small compliment to pay a teenager or any MVP in your life.

Not surprisingly Jeremy routinely gets this kind of respect from his mom and so he is an engaged, happy teenager. When his mom began letting him learn about driving, he felt heard and understood as a human being, instead of marginalized with a "wait until you're older" dismissal. By the time his bus driver fainted, Jeremy had become quite experienced at jumping into the driver's seat. He had practiced adjusting the mirrors, putting in the key, turning the car off and on, engaging the transmission, getting his bearings—checking what was to the side, in front and behind him—then actually pressing the accelerator and brake. We wish older drivers paid such close attention to those important details!

> The trick in hiring the right person is to mine a candidate's background for a track record of performance similar to what you need in this job.

Instead of looking at Jeremy's interest in cars as inappropriate or too dangerous to develop at his age, his mom took the opportunity to allow her son to do something a little risky (or a little taboo) that, in the end, built confidence in both of them. Jeremy and his mom were both learning

RECRUIT / TOOL #17: GET SOMEONE READY

in small steps that added up to a huge amount of confidence when it was tested in a life and death situation.

Opportunities for your team to test their skills and shine don't always come along conveniently or as planned. Routinely ask your team members to work on projects that develop skills they'll need for larger projects. The goal of the leader is to find and develop other leaders, but the only way to do that is to continue to provide opportunities for your team to do more every day. Find ways to encourage them to take on more responsibility—particularly doing the things they think that they're not "ready" for yet.

## How to Recruit a Team of Heroes

Every successful leader tells us that one of the hardest jobs you ever face is hiring and managing people. How do we find the right folks and evaluate whether they're the right ones for the job? The answer lies deep in Jeremy's story because it's at the heart of why he so instantly got the job done right.

Here's the non-intuitive lesson. The best person for any role that is supporting you is not necessarily the friendliest or most attractive person. Contrary to popular leadership literature, it's not necessarily someone you'd be the first to want to go to dinner with. It's not even necessarily someone who can speak eloquently in a job interview. If you hire that person, they may look and act great—or become a good friend—but are they really the best person for the job? You're subconsciously recruiting a pal to hang out with, which wasn't exactly your objective. The real test is to find a way to see how this person has behaved in the past when bad situations hit the proverbial fan. When we have asked experienced managers why they fail to hire people who last

**ADMIRED**

in their roles they admit it's because they were too easily enamored of appearances or fancy resumes, rather than investigating whether the person had actual experience doing exactly what would be expected of them in this role.

I (Bonita) interviewed a corporate manager, Bill, whose company had always asked job candidates to describe how they would handle a hypothetical situation if it arose (rather than asking what they had actually done to handle a similar situation). There is a dangerously big difference between those two approaches to interviews. I told Bill that his company must have hired a lot of people who were great at describing hypothetical situations, and asked if they were they any good at getting work done? Bill was shocked at my question, as if I had read his mind. "No," he frowned. "We had to shut down the operation because it didn't get results."

## Ask What They *Did*, Not What They *Would Do*

The trick in hiring the right person is to mine a candidate's background to look for a track record of performance similar to what you need in this job. Ask specific questions about what they've done in the past, to demonstrate their competence, talent, skill, or even aptitude to learn.

We're not suggesting that you can or should fill every position with experts, but you must look for some past behavior in that person that can be repeated in the job you're offering. Psychologists call this *behavioral interviewing* because there's overwhelming evidence that people tend to do what they've done in the past over and over again for many complex reasons that have to do with nature and nurture. Look hard and long at what that person has done that looks very similar to the abilities needed to succeed in this new venture.

## RECRUIT / TOOL #17: GET SOMEONE READY

The bottom line is that, even though Jeremy had never driven a bus in his life—or even a car in traffic!—he nevertheless saved the day. He performed well in a crisis, not because he was good at imagining a hypothetical one, but because he'd practiced performing the basics of the task successfully *many times* before. That's what you're looking for when recruiting the best people to your team.

ADMIRED

# Putting It to Work for You

To find the right person to support you in your goal:

What are the tasks and the attitudes the person will need to hold in the job.

.................................................................................................

.................................................................................................

.................................................................................................

.................................................................................................

.................................................................................................

.................................................................................................

.................................................................................................

.................................................................................................

.................................................................................................

.................................................................................................

# Tool #18: Don't Play the Blame Game

Nothing kills creativity faster than blame. When something goes wrong, it's natural to feel defensive and easy to point a finger at others—our colleagues, clients, partner, or even the boss. But this knee-jerk behavior leads to resentment among colleagues, a negative work environment, and most importantly, it ignores a golden opportunity for innovation. Instead, focus on creating an environment that supports and rewards creative thinking by stopping the blame game. It doesn't really matter who is to blame, if you can create something that is greater than the problem you need to solve.

"Without fiascos, you will never succeed." That's what billionaire, Ingvar Kamprad, believes. For decades the innovative founder of Swedish furniture giant IKEA has been among the most wealthy on Forbes 400 list. We sat with him in the cafeteria of an IKEA store in Switzerland feasting on Swedish meatballs.

"People don't like to take risks," he frowned. "So when a mistake has been made, people blame the other guy for what went wrong," he grinned and pointed at the people sitting on both sides of him. "That's why there needs to be a leader who's willing to take responsibility." It's uncomfortable to make mistakes in public, but that's the only way to improve at what you do. People fear voicing a "bad idea" or being responsible for a failure, but taking action in the face of that fear is the difference between being good and becoming great.

"Only when we are sleeping do we not take risks!" Kamprad smirked. "There are few people who have made as many mistakes as I have—too many. But it's a question of always having a possibility to correct the mistakes you've made. You're always allowed to make mistakes. And we do, everyday."

ADMIRED

## A Chance to Innovate

Getting comfortable making mistakes in front of your MVPs is central to becoming admired. When your teammates, your boss, or your customers

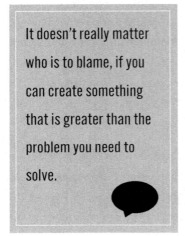

It doesn't really matter who is to blame, if you can create something that is greater than the problem you need to solve.

see you recognize the failure and then turn it into an opportunity to create something better, that builds trust and respect. As a leader, strive to create an environment that supports mistakes and the people who make them. Don't let your staff run and hide, but air the misstep and open up a conversation—either with an individual or with the group—about what you can do to not only rectify the situation, but what weakness the failure may reveal that you've never noticed before or what opportunity it provides to create something even stronger.

Business icon and former head of GE Jack Welch told me once about the time, early in his career, when he blew up a factory. But what could have been a devastating turn in his career became a powerful education. At the time Welch was the manufacturing head of a pilot plant producing a new plastic. Twenty-seven years old and only working a short-time since earning his PhD, Welch admits he thought he was "some smart fellow." One day he was sitting in his office, across the way from the power plant, when he heard an incredible explosion. He looked out his window and saw billowing smoke, the roof in pieces, and shattered glass everywhere. His heart sank with dread, but Welch soon found out that incredibly, no one had been hurt. Now all he had to do was explain this to the higher ups. The drive to Bridgeport, Connecticut to explain the situation to his boss's boss was the longest ride (following the longest night) of Welch's young career. He really didn't know what would happen, but was mentally preparing for the worst.

Instead of being lambasted and sent packing though, the executive calmly asked him what had happened and if he knew how to fix it. Welch remembers him as a sweetheart of a man—a chemical engineer and former MIT professor—who was a great influence on him. That day he taught Welch the importance of never kicking somebody when they're down. This exec didn't blame young Welch for destroying the factory or make him feel ashamed for having failed. Instead he wanted to know if Welch could figure out the answer to the problem and encouraged him to take his time, get it right, and move forward. Welch felt lucky to have received the guidance and the support he needed to learn from this expensive mistake. And in the end, GE had stuck with a challenging innovation project that resulted in a better product than their risk-adverse competitors.

Hopefully you never have to blow up a building, but you can create the same environment Welch's boss did that day. When mistakes happen, and they always do if you're trying to do anything innovative, don't resort to blame. Recruit your MVPs to the solution. Take the opportunity to innovate and create something larger and more powerful than you had before.

ADMIRED

### Leave Blame to the Politicians

While mud-slinging may feel useful in the heat of the moment, it is best left for the unique world of politics and not at home or work. Every election battle is a classic case of the blame game. President Obama joked about this strange dynamic at the 2012 Correspondent's Dinner, an annual black-tie roast with the press, Hollywood stars, and Washington insiders. He said he'd been cautioned about blaming too much of the nation's financial crisis on prior administrations. "But for the record, I'd like to point out that was a practice started by my predecessor!"

RECRUIT / TOOL #18: DON'T PLAY THE BLAME GAME

# Putting it to Work for You

When you blame others (rightly or wrongly) you're giving away your power and control over getting it fixed. Regardless of fault, how could you get back in action mode to solve the problem?

......................................................................................................

......................................................................................................

......................................................................................................

How could you use this problem as an opportunity to innovate and make the whole situation or product even better next time?

......................................................................................................

......................................................................................................

......................................................................................................

192

# 14

## EXCITE

Successful leaders know how to discover what lights their own fire, how to identify the fire in others, and how to keep that flame burning—how to excite progress toward your goal. We'll finish this book with some strategic ways to keep yourself and your MVPs excited. Tool #19 encourages you to embrace the ways in which you're different from your competitors and use them to add more value to the important people in your life. Tool #20 stresses the importance of finding your own voice and using it to have a positive impact. And lastly, tool #21 explores how the age-old practice of storytelling is crucial to getting your point across and holding your MVPs' attention

ADMIRED

# Tool #19: Be Different

Award-winning author Dave Eggers wanted to help kids find a love of writing and literature in San Francisco's Mission District. He wanted to create a place that was kid-focused, non-judgmental, and close to the local school. His strong community of writers also wanted a place to get together and write during the day. He thought these friends could help to connect the author community with grade school kids who needed one-on-one help with their homework. So he signed a year lease on a storefront, filled it with desks and chairs, and put out a sign saying, "free tutoring". Unfortunately, no one came. To make matters worse the government said that their building was zoned for retail—not non-profit education—so they had to run a store or leave.

To comply with the city regulation, Mr. Eggers could have sold textbooks or pencils like any other tutoring center. Instead, he decided to do what he encouraged his students to do: get creative. If he had to run a store, why not sell pirate supplies: wooden-legs, compasses, and eye-patches? Everything a pirate would need in one shop. In the back of the store, he built a pirate ship with tables suitable for studying. Next, he teamed up with a teacher, Ninive Calegari, to advise them on what her students needed most and help build trust in the school community. He didn't need the "free tutoring" sign anymore. The neighborhood wanted to know what this new shop was all about.

If you walk into the 826 Valencia Street tutoring center today, it is abuzz with 6- to 18-year-olds doing homework and writing stories and books. The center prints students' stories in books that the public can purchase, making the kids published authors. 826 Valencia has grown to many other cities and now tutors about 30,000 students with 6,000 volunteers.

## Let Them Show Their True Colors

826 Valencia Street could have been like any other tutoring center, cutting costs and making ends meet, but because they were forced to open a commercial store, they found their uniqueness. Dave Eggers didn't just start this amazing tutoring center because he wanted to share his love of writing with the world. His teacher mother raised him to value his combined love of teaching, writing, and community building. He learned to honor his uniqueness and to feel confident that it would help him make an impact on the world.

When we interviewed 826 Valencia's CEO Gerald Richards, we were most interested in how they got 6,000 people to volunteer on a regular basis. Mr. Richards said not only is it important to have a unique product offering but you must treat your employees and volunteers in a unique way as well. Give your volunteers a voice in how they can approach their work or improve the product. Some of the volunteers offered to do a fund-raiser by seeing who could grow the longest mustache. This is not something Richards could have dreamed up, but it excited the volunteers and added value to the company.

And don't just tell them you appreciate them; show them by taking the time to find out how they want to contribute. Build recognition and rewards around each volunteer's unique gifts. Mr. Richards advised that gifts and support can come in different ways. We can sometimes be so focused on getting money, that we miss the free expertise or talent someone is offering us. So be appreciative of whatever form gifts come in.

## Show Off Your Uniqueness

What do you do if you are not the boss and can't turn your office into a pirate ship? Find a way to make your work a unique product. I (Bonita) was faced with this when working at Bank of America on a project to make the compensation programs more associated with performance. Working on a team with 20 other compensation professionals, I was able to differentiate my work by automating it and branding the computer program I developed with the name "The Market Analyzer." Automating the analysis allowed the managers to look at the data from many perspectives and find which jobs needed compensation adjustments. Making the product unique—giving it a name and personality—allowed the managers to become more independent and effective at compensating their employees and had more overall impact.

Don't just tell them you appreciate them; show them by taking the time to find out how they want to contribute.

You are unique. Not only do you have a unique set of talents and abilities. You also have a unique set of interests shaped by moments of glory and pain. Because your perspective on life is molded by your unique set of experiences and your community and contacts are unique, you have a set of opportunities like no one else's. In a world that wants us to be uniform, it can be hard to nurture and encourage our uniqueness. Yet somewhere in your unique combination of talents, interests, perspectives, and community is a gift that you have to give the world where you can have true impact.

**EXCITE / TOOL #19: BE DIFFERENT**

## Know Your Competition

In our work as coaches, we often hear executives argue that they have no "real" competition. They're surprised when we respond that, if that's true, they should be frightened for two reasons. First, having no competition means there are no customers. There's no market for what you have so that's why no one else has made it work. The second and more likely reason you don't see competition is that you've not taken the time necessary to understand where those dollars are being spent elsewhere. You're competing for attention and often money, so where are customers investing those resources right now? Many executives dismiss competitors as irrelevant or inferior, and lament the ignorance of the wayward customers who buy Brand X. That's not wise. To ignore what the other guys are doing misses a huge opportunity to win admiration and respect with customers.

ADMIRED

# Putting to use at your work

What makes you or your product differentiated?

.......................................................................................................

.......................................................................................................

.......................................................................................................

.......................................................................................................

What value do your MVPs perceive from others that is different from the value you offer?

.......................................................................................................

.......................................................................................................

.......................................................................................................

.......................................................................................................

.......................................................................................................

Why should they switch to use you or your product instead?

.......................................................................................................

.......................................................................................................

.......................................................................................................

.......................................................................................................

.......................................................................................................

## EXCITE / TOOL #19: BE DIFFERENT

How could you provide more value?

How could you add more fun, convenience, and/or ease of use?

Craft your value-add pitch. In 25 words or less, what value can you offer your MVP?

ADMIRED

# Tool #20: Get Heard

Benjamin Zander, conductor of the Boston Philharmonic, is on a constant quest to bring out the very best from his musicians. Some say he has never given the same performance twice. In an interview in his home, he shared with us the essence of what his work is all about. "The meaning of 'symphonia' is 'voices sounding together,'" he explained. "So the job of the conductor is to make sure every voice is heard. Not only heard, but beautifully expressed. It is very easy to tell people 'you shut up, and you shut up, and you shut up and then this person will be heard' but that is not what music is about at all. It's about getting people to be fully expressed—passionately engaged in giving their all—and still enabling everybody else to be heard too."

It's unfortunate that we don't have a conductor for our lives, assuring that we all get heard. There's a craft to being heard even when all the voices are in full symphony. Ironically, a great way to get heard is to help *other* voices get heard.

Being heard and recognized for your potential and achievements is a constant challenge for most people who are quietly doing their job, so it's time that you set your sights on becoming better known for your unique talents. Volunteer for projects that give your contributions more visibility at work, in your community, and wherever people gather to talk about your topic.

## EXCITE / TOOL #20: GET HEARD

## Find Your Voice

You would think that a news reporter would have a natural talent for this, but even media experts have to start out in the trenches to learn how to get just the right kind of attention in their profession. Ira Glass, the host and creator of the award winning radio program, *This American Life*, found himself in exactly this position while still a fledgling reporter for NPR. He'd started with the organization at only 19 years old, but by 26 he was—quite literally—attempting to match both his voice and content to the conventional NPR style. The results were disappointing, and he was frustrated.

Yet instead of giving up on radio journalism altogether, or staying on as a mediocre correspondent, Glass went back to the beginning. He reflected on the reason he'd had a passion for broadcast journalism in the first place and a key realization occurred. "You get into [creative] work because you have good taste, so the reason you know you're not doing your best work is *because* of that good taste."

Glass isn't minimizing that feeling of disappointment, though. In fact, he believes it is at exactly that point where most people give up. "But if I can say with all my heart to people who are at that point, everyone I've ever met who does interesting, creative work went through a period of years of making work that they knew wasn't their best," he emphasized. "It didn't have that special thing that we wanted it to have. The most important possible advice I can say to you if you're at that phase, or just entering that phase, is that it's normal."

Glass kept faith in himself and his passion for journalism and ended up with his own unique show. Since 1995, he has been producing *This American Life*, which combines both fictional and true stories, as well as investigations on often overlooked or ignored subjects, ranging from the deeply personal to the relevant political. But how exactly did Glass do it?

**ADMIRED**

How does one move beyond that frustrating "I want to do better work than what I'm doing" phase?

Glass' answer is simple: you have to do it a lot. In fact, he recommends putting yourself on a deadline so that every week or every month, you complete a project. It's best if you have someone who's expecting work from you. Even if it's not someone who pays you, be in a situation where you have to turn out the work. It is only by going through a huge volume of work that you'll close that gap, and begin creating a product that matches your ambitions.

Glass' program has become wildly successful, boasting 1.7 million listeners a week, spun off a TV show on Showtime, and earned him the prestigious Peabody and duPont awards to boot. But what's more, the show has created value beyond Glass himself, becoming a platform to launch the careers of others (like award-winning author David Sedaris who was first heard reading an essay on the program) and eliciting tangible change.

In 2011, Glass earned the George Polk Award in Radio Reporting for an hour-long report that revealed shockingly severe punishments doled out by a county drug court judge in Georgia. Following the airing of that episode (entitled "Very Tough Love"), Georgia's Judicial Qualifying Commission filed fourteen ethical misconduct charges against the judge and within weeks of the filing of charges, she stepped down from the bench and agreed never to seek other judicial offices.

None of that would have been possible if Glass hadn't had the tenacity to keep working until he created the right forum for his voice and method.

## Create a New Platform for Creativity

An innovative startup, Threadless, has also discovered this in a very different way. They have become curators for a platform that provides new artists with a marketplace where they can share their work with the public. Co-founders Jake Nickell and Jacob DeHart started a website with only $1,000 of their own money, where burgeoning artists and designers could submit original work that users could vet and vote on. Winning designs would get selected and printed on tee shirts every couple of months. Designers would get paid and have their work find instant audience and distribution.

Ironically, a great way to get heard is to help *other* voices get heard

Just four years after beginning, they were printing shirts every week. By 2008, Threadless was featured on the cover of *Inc. Magazine* as "The Most Innovative Small Company in America." In the corresponding article, Karim Lakhani, a professor at Harvard Business School was quoted as saying: "Threadless completely blurs that line of who is a producer and who is a consumer. The customers end up playing a critical role across all its operations: idea generation, marketing, sales forecasting. All that has been distributed."

Ultimately Threadless has created an artistic community, representing another example of an organization that found its voice by empowering others to be heard.

Both Threadless and Ira Glass' *This American Life* are examples of how much attention you can get when you give recognition to others. You receive visibility when you make others visible. Success and admiration are ultimately about impact, about building something bigger than

# ADMIRED

ourselves. How can you not only soar in your own life, but help others do the same? When you empower people to let their voices be heard, to make their own unique, creative imprint, they shine *and* admire you for it.

EXCITE / TOOL #20: GET HEARD

## Give Recognition

The best way to *be recognized* is to *give recognition*. How can you find public ways to acknowledge others in the most sincere and meaningful ways? A brilliant example is the passing of the torch as a build-up to the Olympics. Every individual who carries it across the host country gains "ownership" of the world-class event, and recognition for themselves, their organizations, and their communities. The impact is exponential.

Like this Olympic event, organizations and companies who recognize their customers and community leaders can benefit in ways that are much better than advertising. I (Mark) was honored to receive a Lifetime Achievement Award from the Institute for Entrepreneurial Leadership at John F. Kennedy University. But what impressed me most was how the award I received acknowledged so many other incredible people long before it reached me.

First, the award was named after Chuck Smith, the remarkable leader of ATT, who's made a huge contribution to the careers and community causes throughout his tenure. All of those stakeholders got credit for the honor. Second, the award was submitted to the Library of Congress, for special recognition, which further highlights the great work of all the people who are served by, work for or who sponsor the Institute itself. Third, the award was recognized by the local members of Congress, who provided a proclamation about the event--bringing visibility to their offices and to their constituencies. Fourth, the award was used as a launching pad for a new fraternal organization at colleges across America that focuses on entrepreneurs and education. The Institute could have handed out one award, and instead made it more valuable to hundreds of people whose lives were be touched by it.

How can you get more leverage for the recognition that you give your MVPs, and in turn, have all that reflect well on the causes and communities that matter to you most?

ADMIRED

# Putting it to Work for You

Think about your 3 to 5 main objectives, how could you create a public way to give others recognition for helping to achieve those goals and values?

...........................................................................................................

...........................................................................................................

...........................................................................................................

...........................................................................................................

...........................................................................................................

How could you create an event, competition, or publication in which as many people as possible could be recognized for their efforts?

...........................................................................................................

...........................................................................................................

...........................................................................................................

...........................................................................................................

...........................................................................................................

# Tool #21: What's Your Story?

To make a lasting impression, you need to share a personal story that makes an emotional connection with people—an authentic narrative that describes why you care and what you believe in an openhearted, down-to-earth way. Since prehistoric times, the human brain has been hardwired to remember stories heard around the campfire, giving storytellers a huge advantage over anyone armed solely with facts, figures and logic. Ever notice how people listen to anyone who starts to tell a joke—even if it's a really bad one—but they'll ignore a list of the five most important points? That's the primal brain taking charge.

"Telling your story is the most important thing you can learn to do to become believable and remembered," producer Peter Guber told us in his private box at a Golden State Warriors game. Guber should know: He's CEO of Mandalay Entertainment and has been telling great stories for decades. He owns the Oakland-based basketball team, along with professional baseball teams, a casino, and has run a movie studio and a record label (remember the band Kiss?).

Peter Guber has bet his wallet on transforming the world with stories. He produced compelling movies like *The Kids Are All Right*, *The Color Purple*, *Gorillas in the Mist*, *Soul Surfer*, and *Rain Man*. He's taken on intense themes of discrimination, poverty, racism, autism, and sexism—controversial issues expressed in entertaining stories that shine a light on subjects in a way that can change attitudes in the most difficult circumstances.

**ADMIRED**

## Stories Help Us Connect

In *Soul Surfer*, a true story about a world-class surfer who lost an arm in a shark attack, the audience feels the acute suffering of this beautiful young woman. Her passion for surfing—the only thing she ever wanted to do with her life—seemed doomed. At some level, we can all relate to feeling hopeless, cheated of our dream. The protagonist in *Soul Surfer* not only lost her shot at being extraordinary in the way she had always imagined, she was also humiliated by her appearance and her inability to be self-sufficient. She eventually embraces her passion so deeply that she becomes extraordinary in a new way—not only as an athlete, but also as a leader who inspires others who have been handicapped to achieve *their* greatest potential despite all odds. This narrative underscores a deep vulnerability and a question all of us face in some way at some point: should we wallow in self-pity or use what we have to energize and build a different, more adventurous future.

"When I look at the last few years of my life, and the times when I'd failed, it was most often because I'd forgotten to tell the story or because I had the wrong story. When I was moved, I was moved by the right story," Guber said. When he shared that story with audiences that could appreciate and benefit from it—paid it forward, as Guber says—"I was often the winner even when I was advocating someone else's story." Stories work even when they're not your story as long as they are relevant to the audience and you believe in them.

"I realized that it came down to being able to take all those facts and data that I know so well, and orchestrate them into an emotional offering so that audiences could metabolize them. You have to convert the information so it becomes resonant, memorable, and actionable. My epiphany was to recognize that the ability to tell stories is innate. Your story is in you, just waiting to be unleashed."

## Anyone Can Tell a Great Story

The secret to telling a great story, says Peter Guber, "is to recognize that the narrative has to be interesting to the audience and not just interesting to you. And the way to do that is to be interested in your audience rather than just be interesting," he smiled. The biggest compliment you can pay anyone is to talk about something that is meaningful to them but that matters to you just as much. People can feel if there's a difference.

"Stories are a misunderstood and underutilized asset, and they aren't just the 'soft' stuff. I spent all these years doing stories and now the story is the story," Guber laughed. "Stories aren't the icing on the cake; they are the cake! If you're going into a room with someone, how do you make your intention clear? How can you inspire them to believe that what you care about is also something they care about deeply?"

"If it's not clear," explains Guber, "your audience isn't going to know what you're talking about because they need to know why you're talking about what you're talking about. What's your call to action? What does it have to do with the people in the room? You have to be authentic right from the start of your story. People get that. Language is a more recent technology. Your body language, your eyes, your energy will come through to your audience before you even start speaking. The portal into people's heart is being interested in them. And when you emotionalize your story, they're going to keep them engaged and *pay it forward*," Guber advises. In other words, your audience will share your story with others and market the ideas you're putting out there. "An open heart is the greatest palette to deliver a story that ever existed."

ADMIRED

## Hero with a Thousand Faces

Author Joseph Campbell spent his career studying the world's greatest stories from dozens of civilizations throughout the ages. He discovered that every narrative has the same ingredients and you can use that recipe to develop your own powerful story.

**1. The Journey:** Great stories start with a hero whose normal life is disrupted by a big problem that launches her on a mission she was reluctant to take or that took her by surprise. During the journey, the hero must surmount at least three major obstacles that seem impossible. When you think about your story, what mission were you called (or compelled or forced) to do unexpectedly, and what 2 to 3 obstacles seemed the most daunting?

**2. The Setting:** We all have five senses, maybe six, but most narratives fail to turn on any of them. One way to breathe life into your story is to describe the place in which the problem occurred so people can picture it or even feel it. Think of ways to add as many details as you can in your story about how the people and things looked to you. Describe the weather, the sounds, textures and smells--these details light up the senses of the listener.

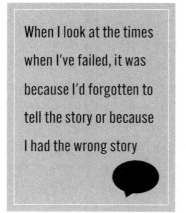

> When I look at the times when I've failed, it was because I'd forgotten to tell the story or because I had the wrong story

**3. The Haunting:** Every great story has a hero haunted by a past experience or handicap that he doesn't feel comfortable revealing to others. The most interesting hero is one who is not only fighting the adversary, but also a war with himself. We can all relate to getting in our way. In Greek mythology, if the hero had the humility and vulnerability

## EXCITE / TOOL #21: WHAT'S YOUR STORY?

to admit his flaws, it was a happy ending. If he refused to admit his past failures, then the myth would end in tragedy. Audiences love to hear about the insecurities and setbacks of successful people because they can empathize. What fears can you share that make your story more emotional and believable?

**4. The Audience:** Scientists have long established that your left brain controls rational thought and data, while the right influences emotional duties. The most powerful way to impress your audience with each of your key messages is to marry every technical piece of data with a personal story that makes it memorable. When we were launching a program for earthquake preparedness, we talked about two heroes and how one saved her family and the other didn't. The difference between the two were the tools and tactics that we wanted our employees to remember. How can you marry every data point that you need to sell with a story that makes it easy to remember and worth caring about?

**5. The Adversaries:** During the hero's journey, the protagonist will meet at least three characters: First, a bad guy or gang. Second, a seemingly innocent, friendly, and helpful Judas-like character who purposely or accidentally make things worse. Third, a Yoda-like person who at first seems to be an odd distraction. This character is a guide who helps you find your way, but only if you have the open-hearted humility to listen. Who mentored you, and who helped or hurt you? What role would you like to the recruit the audience to play in creating the solution to your problem? How can you make the audience a hero?

ADMIRED

# Putting it to Work for You

Peter Guber urges us to embrace a campfire mindset. Think about your next meeting and approach it in a new way. This time craft a story. Start with a narrative about why your project matters to you and why it can connect with your coworkers or a market in a personal way that your team cares about.

What behavior change do you want from your MVPs? Why is that behavior important?

......................................................................................................................

......................................................................................................................

......................................................................................................................

What event happened in your life or someone else's life that illustrates the importance of that behavior?

......................................................................................................................

......................................................................................................................

......................................................................................................................

## EXCITE / TOOL #21: WHAT'S YOUR STORY?

Who is your hero? How does your story touch the lives of employees or teammates and customers in a new or better way? Bank CEO Christian Claussen noticed that when call center executives were reminded of the personal stories of the families who needed a home, they were much more friendly and effective in helping those customers fill out mortgage applications. What stories of people can you share that make your narrative more meaningful?

# Epilogue

If you've ever had a child refuse to follow directions—no matter how influential you may have thought you are—you realize there is no such thing as control over other people. Whenever I think I'm "motivating" someone else, the truth is that they're choosing to be influenced based on their own beliefs, passions, past experiences, or fears even if they don't realize it. They're following their urges based on how well I can connect with what they value, not what anyone else may believe is important, for better or for worse.

I was bringing our daughter, Vanessa, home from school one afternoon and remember feeling frustrated because she was refusing to take a class we had signed her up for. She was 8 at the time, and has always been a cooperative child, sweet and generous beyond her years. But she had drawn the line this time and wouldn't budge. It was something we wanted her to do and we were certain that she'd love it. There is no one in the world more important to us than Vanessa. We only want "what's best for her" (based on our values and beliefs) in every aspect of her life.

Our little girl stood there resolute in the doorway, her golden hair spotlighted by the afternoon sun. She smiled, hands on hips, in her pink and white floral spring dress with knee socks, shaking her braided ponytail back and forth in disapproval. She wasn't angry; she was just clear about her position on the matter and convinced that dad was misguided.

In a vain attempt to persuade her, I kneeled so I could look straight into those killer baby blue eyes. "Honey, this is going to be really fun," I begged. "There is no doubt in my mind that you're going to like it."

Vanessa sighed like a parent who knew better. She put her hand on my

# EPILOGUE

shoulder reassuringly as if I were now the grade-schooler.

"You are the best daddy in the whole world!" She gave me a hug. "But you aren't the boss of my *likes*," she said, clarifying my role. "You're the boss of taking care of me."

My heart skipped a beat. This kid has always been a wise, old soul. She mentors me whenever I become arrogant enough to believe I'm in charge of *everything*. You can't be the boss of someone else's likes—it's pointless to demand to be valued or admired. It has to be earned. With the best of intentions, we often attempt to control the passions of the most valued people in our lives and work.

> You can't be the boss of someone else's likes— it's pointless to demand to be valued or admired. It has to be earned.

I'm not recommending lack of discipline or laissez faire leadership. The best military commanders know that regular troops turn into heroes not because you gave orders but because each soldier knew why the mission mattered and cherished that vision as their own. As parents, coworkers, or bosses, we're accountable for many essential responsibilities, but we often confuse that authority with being in charge of everything. As leaders, our job is to inspire action and give guidance and tools to support the most valuable people in our work and our lives.

But we don't control anyone else's values. Our children are given to us on a short-term lease—and our best employees and closest friends are volunteers—they aren't required to be loyal. The best people don't have to stick with us to pursue their dreams.

Vanessa chose a path that day that took many of the best aspects of what

## ADMIRED

we were recommending as parents and combined them with what she loved. And because she was doing something she deeply cared about, she owned it, and recruited classmates to join her. Together they performed so brilliantly that she was admired, respected, and valued by her teachers, teammates (and parents!) for what matters most.

If you want to be admired for something meaningful—and double your value to the most valuable people—then turn up the oxygen in your life. Find a way to breathe air into the passions and values of your MVPs. When you appreciate what's valuable to you first, then seek sincerely to understand and connect with what drives the people who matter to you with depth and clarity, success is inevitable.

# Appendix: Research for Admired

For this book, we conducted original primary research on a statistically representative sample of Americans in two studies. The first survey asked participants to write-in responses to report which five leaders they admire, what companies they admire and, most important for this book, why they made those choices. From those results, we found 27 traits, 20 of which were very similar to those found in Jim Kouzes and Barry Posner's research (2002; 2003). These two thought leaders have conducted research since the 1980s to determine what characteristics people would be willing to follow in their leaders.

We wanted to know something crucial to your success: How do those 27 traits apply to you as an individual? What do you want to be admired for in comparison with the leaders and companies you most admire? How do these traits impact your level of engagement and enjoyment at work, or how much time you spend on goals and meaningful activities? Are you valued by your boss, your company, and your family, and do you believe they value you? Do you know what they value?

We conducted a second survey of about 1,000 Americans in which we asked for all that detail and more, as you'll see in the following pages. We also captured demographic information, including age, gender, and employment status.

## ADMIRED

As a baseline, here are the 20 characteristics listed by kouzes and Posner (2002). Many researchers have used these characteristics as a basis for their studies. Since these 20 were similar to what we found in our own write-in survey, we used all 20 in our larger 1,000-person study, in addition to seven additional traits that emerged in our survey.

1. honest
2. forward-looking
3. competent
4. inspiring
5. intelligent
6. fair-minded
7. broad-minded
8. supportive
9. straightforward
10. dependable
11. cooperative
12. determined
13. imaginative
14. ambitious
15. courageous
16. caring
17 mature
18. loyal
19. self-controlled
20. independent

Our respondents added an additional seven elements which were

1. cause driven/moral
2. decisive
3. resilient
4. generous & charitable
5. family focused
6. fun-loving & friendly
7. quality focused

Arsenault (2004) conducted a survey asking respondents to rank-order Kouzes and Poser's 20 characteristics, as well as indicate their age. Results of this survey showed that all four cohorts ranked honesty as the number one characteristic.

Powell (2005) also based his study on Kouzes and Poser's work and found statistically significant differences between the three generations

## APPENDIX: RESEARCH FOR ADMIRED

(Boomers, Gen X, and Gen Y) for the 20 characteristics studied

1. Boomers ranked dependability, honesty, fair-mindedness, and broad-mindedness significantly higher than other attributes

2. Gen X ranked dependability, honesty, and fair-mindedness most important.

3. The Gen Y participants did not show much variation in their rankings of the 20 characteristics.

Sessa et al. (2007) also examined most desired leadership attributes, using a set of 40 "leadership components." They found significant differences between generational cohorts in 6 out of the top 12 attributes determined to be important for leaders:

1. credible                4. focused

2. listens well            5. dedicated

3. farsighted              6. optimistic

Gen Y was the only generation that ranked "dedicated" higher than "credible," which is very similar to "honesty" in the Kouzes and Posner set, indicating a difference in findings between the results of Sessa et al. and Arsenault.

## ADMIRED

In our research, respondents do want an honest leader as well, but more importantly they want them to be able to do the job. For our leaders, we want them to be ambitious and hardworking, intelligent, competent, and caring.

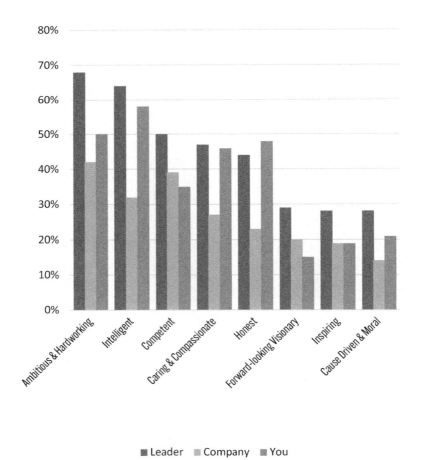

Top 9 Traits Admired in Leaders, Companies, and You

APPENDIX: RESEARCH FOR ADMIRED

## Next 10-18 Traits

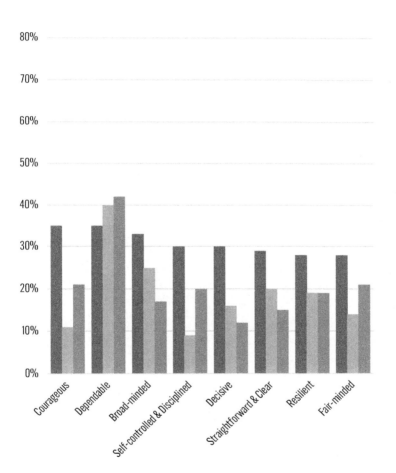

**ADMIRED**

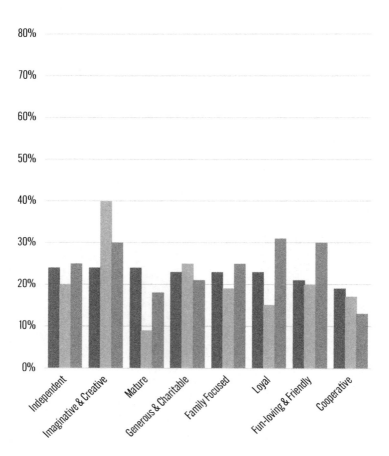

APPENDIX: RESEARCH FOR ADMIRED

## What Do You Admire in Leaders? (*percent*)

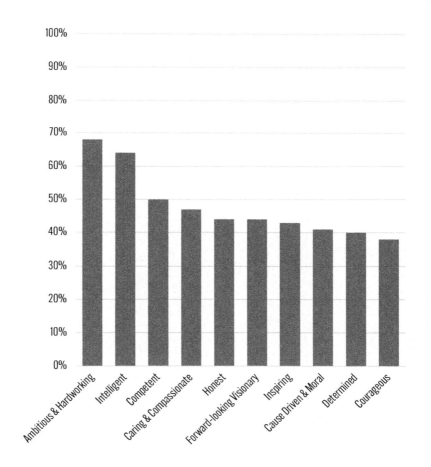

ADMIRED

## What Do You Admire in Companies? (*percent*)

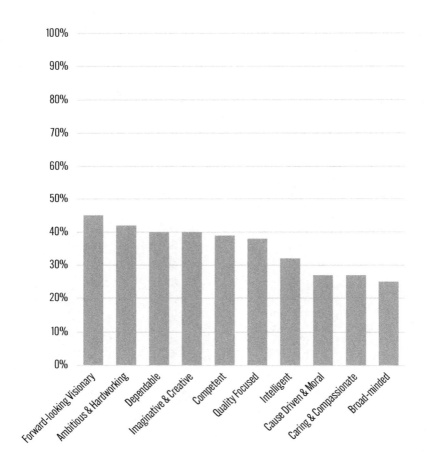

# APPENDIX: RESEARCH FOR ADMIRED

## How Would You Like to Be Admired? (*percent*)

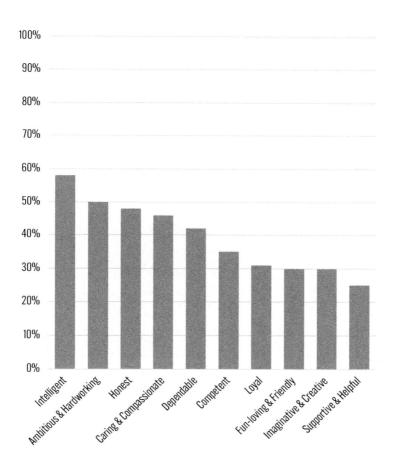

ADMIRED

# Time Spent on Meaningful Projects and Time Spent on Achieving Projects

| Statistics | % of Day Spent on Meaningful Projects | % of Day Spent Achieving Goals |
|---|---|---|
| Mean | 49.21 | 52.63 |
| Median | 50 | 59 |

# Time Spent on Meaningful Projects and Time Spent on Achieving Projects (*by Gender*)

| Gender | Statistics | % of Day Spent on Meaningful Projects | % of Day Spent Achieving Goals |
|---|---|---|---|
| Male | Mean | 46.57 | 52.57 |
| N=414 | Median | 45.5 | 60 |
| Female | Mean | 51.39 | 52.77 |
| N=510 | Median | 56 | 57 |

APPENDIX: RESEARCH FOR ADMIRED

# Time Spent on Meaningful Projects and Time Spent on Achieving Goals (*by Age Group*)

| Age | Statistics | % of Day Spent on Meaningful Projects | % of Day Spent Achieving Goals |
|---|---|---|---|
| 19-25 | Mean | 48.07 | 57.78 |
| N=318 | Median | 46.5 | 61 |
| 26-30 | Mean | 47.18 | 49.21 |
| N=212 | Median | 50 | 50 |
| 31-35 | Mean | 45.69 | 51.51 |
| N=109 | Median | 40 | 50 |
| 36-45 | Mean | 53.77 | 46.94 |
| N=130 | Median | 61 | 48 |
| 46-55 | Mean | 55.41 | 53.75 |
| N=100 | Median | 60 | 54 |
| 56-65 | Mean | 50.24 | 50.51 |
| N=45 | Median | 60 | 60 |
| over 65 | Mean | 43.1 | 57.1 |
| N=10 | Median | 40 | 55 |

**ADMIRED**

# Time Spent on Meaningful Projects and Time Spent on Achieving Projects

| Statistics | % of Day Spent on Meaningful Projects | % of Day Spent Achieving Goals |
|---|---|---|
| Mean | 5.16 | 4.71 |
| Median | 5 | 5 |

# Time Spent on Meaningful Projects and Time Spent on Achieving Projects (*by Gender)*

| Age | Statistics | Engagement | Enjoyment |
|---|---|---|---|
| Male | Mean | 4.89 | 4.48 |
| N=414 | Median | 5 | 5 |
| Female | Mean | 5.37 | 4.89 |
| N=510 | Median | 6 | 5 |

APPENDIX: RESEARCH FOR ADMIRED

# On a Scale of 1-7 How Engaged Are You at Work?
## How Much Do You Enjoy Your Work? (*by Age Group*)

| Age | Statistics | Engagement | Enjoyment |
|---|---|---|---|
| 19–25 | Mean | 4.97 | 4.56 |
| N=318 | Median | 5 | 5 |
| 26–30 | Mean | 5.15 | 4.67 |
| N=212 | Median | 5 | 5 |
| 31–35 | Mean | 5.2 | 4.72 |
| N=109 | Median | 6 | 5 |
| 36-45 | Mean | 5.33 | 4.79 |
| N=130 | Median | 6 | 5 |
| 46-55 | Mean | 5.42 | 5.02 |
| N=100 | Median | 6 | 5 |
| 56-65 | Mean | 5.42 | 4.87 |
| N=45 | Median | 6 | 5 |
| over 65 | Mean | 4.9 | 5 |
| N=10 | Median | 5 | 5 |

**ADMIRED**

# Meaning Matters: Respondents were more likely to be engaged if they found meaning in their work.

|  | % of Day Meaningful | % of Day Achieve Goals | Engagement with Work | Enjoyment of Work |
|---|---|---|---|---|
| % of Day | 1 | .270** | .402** | 394** |
| Meaningful | .270** | 1 | 196** | 195** |
| % of Day | 402** | .196** | 1 | .663** |
| Achieve Goals | .394** | .195** | .663** | 1 |

|  | Boss Values You | What Boss Values | Engagement | Enjoyment |
|---|---|---|---|---|
| Boss | 1 | .359** | .275** | 370** |
| Values You | .359** | 1 | .225** | .248** |
| What Boss | .275** | .225** | 1 | .663** |
| Values | 370** | .248** | .663** | 1 |

APPENDIX: RESEARCH FOR ADMIRED

# What Engaged Workers Want in a Leader

|  | Cooperative |
|---|---|
| Work Enjoyment | .006* |

We found one particular leadership trait-Cooperative-had a correlation (.066) with Work Enjoyment.

|  | Ambitious & Hard-working | Coopera-tive | Honest | Loyal | Straight-forward & Clear | Supportive & Helpful Work |
|---|---|---|---|---|---|---|
| Work Engaged | .074* | .075* | .066* | .078* | .080* | .090** |

We found that these six leadership traits (above) had a high correlation with Work Engagement, particularly if the leader was Supportive and Helpful (.090).

|  | Ambitious & Hard-working | Coopera-tive | Honest | Loyal | Enjoyment |
|---|---|---|---|---|---|
| Meaningful | .088** | .074* | .078* | .097** | .093** |

We found that these five leadership traits (above) had a high correlation with spending time pursuing Meaningful goals, particularly if the leader was Supportive and Helpful (.093).

\* Correlation is significant at the 0.05 level (2-tailed).
\*\* Correlation is significant at the 0.01 level (2-tailed).

ADMIRED

## In your current work/life how do you feel your boss/customer/family values you? On a scale of 1-7

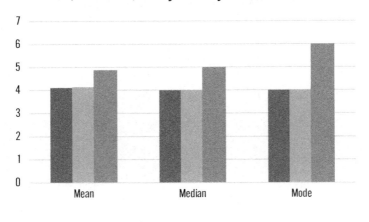

## Do you know what your boss/customer/family values? On a scale of 1-7

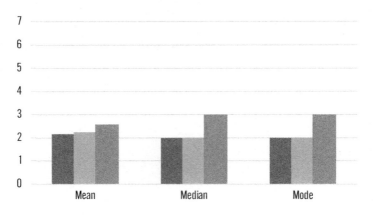

# About the Authors

## Mark C. Thompson

Mark Thompson is ranked the #1 CEO Coach in the World by the Thinkers 50 Leading Global Coaches, the American Management Association and the 2021 Harvard | McLean Institute of Coaching. He is a three time Chairman & CEO and an honored alumnus of Stanford University. Mark is a founder of the Stanford CEO Summit Series, a NY Times bestselling author and the first to be selected as a Global Guru in both the Leadership and Coaching categories. In 2022 Mark is among only six leaders in history to be inducted to the Global Gurus Hall of Fame | Corps d'Elite.

With over 30 years' operating experience, Mark focuses on New CEO Readiness for more than 85 boards of directors. He specializes in high profile leaders, celebrity CEOs and family members from Virgin Group founder Sir Richard Branson, Google founder Larry Page, Amazon

## ADMIRED

founder Jeff Bezos, Pinterest founder Evan Sharp, World Bank CEO Jim Kim, Charles Schwab, Apple founder Steve Jobs and Tony Robbins.

He is a New York Times bestselling author with titles that include: Admired: 21 Ways to Double Your Value; Now, Build a Great Business!: Seven Ways to Maximize Your Profits in Any Market; and Success Built to Last: Creating a Life that Matters.

A leading authority on CEO Readiness, Mark is a co-founder of the legendary Stanford University Realtime Venture Design Lab and cofounding patron of Sir Richard Branson's Entrepreneurship Centres. Previously, he was Charles 'Chuck' Schwab's Chief of Staff and CEO of Schwab.com, he created the first Chief Customer Experience Officer role which is now a world standard.

# ABOUT THE AUTHORS

## Dr. Bonita S. Thompson, Ed.D, MBA

Dr. Bonita Thompson, Ed.D, MBA is New York Times Bestselling Author of Admired: 21 Ways to Double Your Value. She developed the world's first Collaborative Leadership construct in the Chief Learning Officer doctoral program at the University of Pennsylvania in partnership with Harvard University's Kennedy School. She served as Adjunct Faculty for the Advanced Coaching Workshop at Harvard|McLean Hospital Institute of Coaching and John F. Kennedy University. In 2019, she was recognized as Business Leader of the Year at the Harvard Club NYC (GC4W) Global Connections for Women–awarded for her Leadership Innovation and Workforce Reinvention at Bank of America, Levi Strauss, Genentech, Virgin Unite, Varian, Pacific Telesis and The World Bank. Dr. Thompson has been cited by the U.S. Congress and California Department of Education for her groundbreaking project-based learning programs in mathematics.

# CHIEF EXECUTIVE ALLIANCE

## The World's Premier CEO Community

The Chief Executive Alliance is an invitation-only community of Board Members, CEOs, executive candidates and global thought leaders, committed to supporting one another's professional and personal missions for collaborative impact.

**Alan Mulally**
Former CEO, Ford Motor Co.

**Richard Branson**
Founder, Virgin Group

**Charles Schwab**
Founder, Schwab

**Venus Williams**
Olympic Tennis Champion

Learn more and watch weekly CEO interviews & podcasts on www.chiefexecutivealliance.com